PreK

INTERACTIVE

Read-Aloud

ANTHOLOGY with STORIES, RHYMES, AND SONGS

Mc
Graw
Hill
Education

Send all inquiries to:
McGraw-Hill Education
8787 Orion Place
Columbus, OH 43240

ISBN: 978-0-07-666150-3
MHID: 0-07-666150-4

Printed in the United States of America.

1 2 3 4 5 6 7 8 9 RHR 22 21 20 19 18 17 16 15

Contents

Folk Tales, Fairy Tales, and Fables

Introduction 8

Anansi's Dinner Guest An Ashanti Tale 10

The Boy Who Cried Wolf A Fable by Aesop 14

The Bremen Town Musicians A Tale from Germany 16

Brer Rabbit Meets Brer Lion An African American Tale 20

Cinderella A Tale from France 24

City Mouse and Country Mouse A Fable by Aesop 28

The Clever Jackal A Tale from India 31

The Crocodile and the Hen A Tale from Central Africa 35

The Foolish, Timid Rabbit A Tale from India 37

Grandmother Spider Brings the Sun A Cherokee Tale 40

Jack and the Beanstalk A Tale from England 43

The Johnny Cake Boy An Appalachian Tale 47

The Knee-High Man An African American Tale 51

The Lion and the Mouse A Fable by Aesop 54

Little Juan and the Cooking Pot A Tale from Puerto Rico 56

The Little Red Hen A Tale from England 59

Little Red Riding Hood A Tale from Germany 61

Mouse Deer Crosses the River A Tale from Malaysia 64

Now Things Are Worse! A Yiddish Tale 68

Rabbit and Coyote's Big Race A Pueblo Tale 72

The Rooster Who Went to Tío's Wedding A Tale from Cuba 75

The Three Bears A Tale from England 79

The Three Billy Goats Gruff A Tale from Norway 82

The Three Little Pigs A Tale from England 84

Tikki Tikki Tembo A Tale from China 87

Timimoto A Tale from Japan 91

The Tortoise and the Hare A Fable by Aesop 94

The Turtle and the Flute A Tale from Brazil 96

The Voice in Rabbit's House A Masai Tale 99

Mother Goose Rhymes

Introduction 102

Old Mother Goose 104

Jack and Jill 104

Diddle, Diddle, Dumpling 104

Hey! Diddle, Diddle 104

Six Little Mice 105

To Market 105

Rain, Rain, Go Away 105

Pease-Porridge Hot 105

Three Little Kittens 106

The Pumpkin Eater 107

If I Had a Donkey 107

Doctor Foster 107

The Crooked Man 107

Jack Sprat 107

Wee Willie Winkie 108

Little Jack Horner 108

Polly Put the Kettle On 108

It's Raining 108

Mary, Mary, Quite Contrary 108

Ride Away, Ride Away 109

My Black Hen 109

Blow, Wind, Blow! 109

If All the World Was Paper 109

Star Light 109

Little Boy Blue 110

Baa, Baa, Black Sheep 110

1, 2, Buckle My Shoe 110

Tommy Tucker 110

If All the Seas 111

Mary Had a Little Lamb 111

1, 2, 3, 4, 5 111

Roses Are Red 111

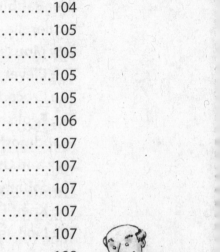

Little Bo-Peep 112

Peter Piper 112

Humpty Dumpty 112

Old Woman 112

Hoddley, Poddley 112

Hickory, Dickory, Dock 113

Pussy-Cat, Pussy-Cat 113

Hot Cross Buns 113

Pat-a-Cake 113

Tweedledum and Tweedledee 114

Three Men in a Tub 114

The Pie 114

Sulkey Sue 114

Old Mother Hubbard 114

Little Miss Muffet 115

Sing a Song of Sixpence 115

Tom, Tom, the Piper's Son 115

The North Wind 116

Hush-a-Bye 116

Ring Around the Rosy 116

Higglety, Pigglety, Pop 116

Simple Simon 117

The Owl 117

One Misty, Moisty Morning 117

Ding, Dong, Bell 117

Jack-a-Nory 118

Georgy Porgy 118

The Bat 118

The Old Woman Who Lived in a Shoe 118

Jack, Be Nimble 119

Bow-Wow 119

Three Blind Mice 119

Going to St. Ives 119

This Is the House That Jack Built 120

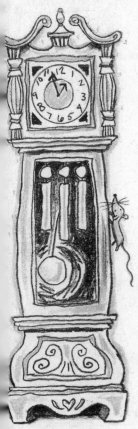

Song Favorites

Introduction 122

1, 2, 3, 4, 5 124

1, 2, Buckle My Shoe 125

A be ce 126

Alphabet Song 127

America 128

America, the Beautiful 129

Apples and Bananas 130

Autumn Leaves 131

Bell Horses 131

Bickle, Bockle 132

Bingo 132

Bounce High, Bounce Low 133

Burn Little Candles 134

Bye 'n' Bye 135

Clap Your Hands 135

Down at the Station 136

Eency Weency Spider 137

Engine, Engine, Number Nine 137

The Farmer in the Dell 138

Five Fat Turkeys 139

Follow Me 140

Go a Tin (Lantern Song) 141

Go Tell It on the Mountain 141

Gogo 142

Good Day Song 143

Hello Song 144

Higglety, Pigglety, Pop 145

The Hokey Pokey 146

Hop, Hop, Hop 147

Hush, Little Baby 147

I Wanna Be a Friend of Yours 148

If You're Happy 149

Jack, Be Nimble 150

Jingle Bells 151

Kum Ba Yah 152

La pequeñita araña (Eency Weency Spider) 153

London Bridge 154

Looby Loo 155

Los pollitos (Little Chickens) 156

Mary Wore Her Red Dress 157

Merrily, We Roll Along 157

Mi cuerpo (My Body) 158

The Muffin Man 159

The Mulberry Bush 160

My Thumbs Are Starting to Wiggle 161

Oats, Peas, Beans, and Barley Grow 162

Old MacDonald Had a Farm 163

Rain, Rain, Go Away 164

Ring Around the Rosy 164

Sally Go 'Round the Sun 165

Sing a Song of Sixpence 166

Six Little Ducks 167

Skip to My Lou 168

Song of Thanksgiving 169

Sweetly Sings the Donkey 169

Teddy Bear 170

Ten in a Bed 171

This Is What I Can Do 172

This Little Light of Mine 173

Three Little Muffins 174

Touch Your Shoulders 175

Twinkle, Twinkle, Little Star 176

We Wish You a Merry Christmas 177

The Wheels on the Bus 178

Yankee Doodle 179

Folk Tales, Fairy Tales, and Fables

Young children love to listen to stories, and few stories are more powerful and engaging than folk tales, fairy tales, and fables. These traditional stories from long ago and far away have much to offer children personally, socially, and intellectually, and have many uses in the classroom.

Traditional tales are an invaluable introduction to the world of reading and literature. Because the stories were passed down orally, they have a pared-down simplicity that helps children develop an understanding of story structure. Repetitive phrases and other features make these stories naturally interactive and memorable.

Folk tales, fairy tales, and fables speak to children's emotional concerns and help to instill important values. Whether the story is about the little pigs who are able to outsmart the big bad wolf, or the slow tortoise whose perseverance helps him win the race, these tales help children develop a sense of how to act in the world.

Traditional tales also introduce children to the world's cultures. The tales in this collection include classics that all children should know. They also introduce important folk characters from around the world. Children will meet such cultural heroes as Anansi, Brer Rabbit, Coyote, and Mouse Deer.

Finally, classic tales are just plain fun. Whether we smile at the cleverness of a Brer Rabbit, chuckle at the family living with their barn animals, or give our hearts to the plight of poor Cinderella, these tales are always immediate and engaging. They are truly the best read-aloud stories in the world.

Using the Interactive Read-Aloud Anthology

Following are additional components and instructional features designed to enhance the read-aloud experience.

Retelling Cards

Each story has a set of three Retelling Cards. These richly illustrated cards feature images from the beginning, middle, and end of the story on one side. On the other side are questions to help guide children to retell the story. The cards should also be displayed while reading the story.

Mother Goose Puppet

As a fun and warm representation of the classic storyteller, the Mother Goose Puppet will draw children into the experience of listening to oral stories. The puppet can be used to ask children questions, to comment on story events, or to act as the narrator in story reenactments.

Wonderful Words

Reading stories aloud presents wonderful opportunities for children to experience rich vocabulary in an engaging context. To take advantage of this opportunity, two to four Wonderful Words are boldfaced in each story. Instructional copy designed to help children understand and use the words appears on the side column.

Listening Comprehension

Questions to ask children while reading the story appear on the side column. They are designed to help children make predictions, understand story structure, make inferences about characters' motivations, and more.

Respond to the Story

Following every story are questions that will help children think about the larger issues in the story and connect the story to their own experiences. There is also an activity that will help children respond to the story using art, writing, movement, and more.

ANANSI'S DINNER GUEST

An Ashanti Tale

WONDERFUL WORD

improved

Define: *Improved* means got better.

Example: Jason's writing has really *improved*.

Ask: What have you *improved* at this year?

Listening Comprehension

How does Anansi feel about sharing his meal with Turtle? How can you tell?

There was hardly anything that Anansi, the spider, liked better than a good meal. One day, he picked some delicious-looking yams from his garden. He cooked them up with his favorite spices.

A mouth-watering smell was coming from Anansi's house when Turtle walked by. "That Anansi sure has **improved** his cooking skills," said Turtle. "And I haven't had a single bite to eat all day."

He walked right over to Anansi's window. "Hello, Anansi!" he called. "I have been walking all day with no food to keep me going. I would be so grateful if you would share your meal with me."

"Good day, Turtle," said Anansi. "How can I say no? Come in."

Now the very last thing Anansi wanted to do was to share his delicious yams. But where he lived, it was considered to be very rude to turn away a dinner guest, especially a hungry and tired one.

Turtle sat right down at the table and reached for some yams. Anansi had to think fast.

"Turtle," he said, "I'm surprised at you! Don't you know better than to come to the table with dirty hands?"

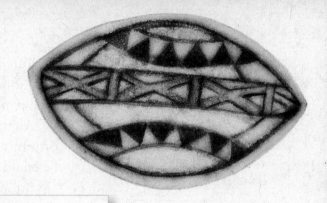

"I beg your pardon, Anansi," said Turtle. He looked down at his hands and saw that they were filthy.

Turtle got up from the table and walked all the way down to the river to clean his hands. By the time he got back to the table, Anansi had eaten half the yams.

"Yum!" said Turtle as he reached for some yams.

"Turtle," said Anansi, "did you not hear me? I said it's not **polite** to come to the table with dirty hands."

Turtle looked down. Sure enough, his clean hands had become dirty from walking back through the mud.

"I beg your pardon, Anansi," he said.

Once again, Turtle got up from the table and walked down to the river to wash himself. This time, on the way back he tiptoed carefully on the grass to keep clean.

He sat back down at the table, his mouth watering from thinking about the yams. But Anansi was just putting the very last of the yams in his mouth. There wasn't a bite left for Turtle to eat!

Turtle was so hungry his stomach was growling. "Anansi tricked me!" he thought. But he got up and said, "Thank you so much for sharing your dinner with me, Anansi. I promise to return the favor some day. The next time you are near my house, please come by for a tasty dinner."

Not long after, Anansi found himself in Turtle's neighborhood. He remembered Turtle's promise. He found Turtle sunning himself on the bank of the river.

"Hello, my good friend, Anansi," said Turtle. "You are just in time to share my delicious evening meal."

Anansi patted his stomach and smiled.

WONDERFUL WORD

polite
Define: *Polite* means to have good manners and be well-behaved.
Example: It is *polite* to wait your turn.
Ask: What is a *polite* way to act at the table?

Listening Comprehension

Why does Anansi ask Turtle to wash his hands? Do you think Anansi really cares about dirty hands?

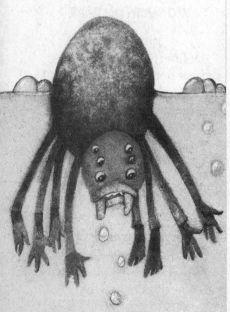

Turtle swam to the bottom of the river and set a table for two. Soon, he came back. "Your food is waiting," he said. "Just follow me."

Anansi jumped in and swam down. When he saw the table brimming with all kinds of meats and fishes and fruits and nuts, he could hardly believe his good luck.

But just as soon as he sat down, he began to float back up to the top of the river. He tried to swim to the table again. But he floated right back up to the top. He was too light to stay down!

Anansi was not one to give up a free meal so easily. He ran around wondering what to do and worried that Turtle would eat everything by the time he returned. Then he had an idea. He grabbed some stones and put them in the pockets of his jacket.

He jumped into the river once again. This time, with the stones in his pockets, he floated easily down. He took his place at Turtle's table.

Just as Anansi reached for his first taste, Turtle said, "In my land, Anansi, we do not wear jackets at the dinner table."

"I beg your pardon, Turtle," said Anansi. He got up to take off his jacket, trying to decide which delicious thing he would eat first.

But as soon as his jacket was off, he floated back up to the surface. He popped out of the water.

"Turtle tricked me!" he said. Anansi could hardly believe that a slow **creature** like Turtle could get the better of him. But when he looked down at Turtle finishing every last bit of his feast, he knew it was true.

WONDERFUL WORD

creature

Define: A *creature* is any human, animal or made-up being.

Example: A mouse is a tiny *creature*.

Ask: Which of the following are *creatures*? (dog, tree, fish, girl, house)

Respond to the Story

Retell: Use the prompts on the back of the Retelling Cards to help children retell the story.

Think About It

1. What do you think of the way Anansi acted toward Turtle? What would you tell Anansi?

2. Do you think Turtle should have tricked Anansi back? Why or why not?

Activity: Have children draw an underwater feast of favorite foods such as the one Turtle sets out for Anansi. Help them to label the foods. They can paint a light blue wash over their drawings or attach light blue tissue paper to make it look like an underwater scene.

The Boy Who Cried Wolf

A Fable by Aesop

There once was a young shepherd boy who spent his days in the hills watching the village sheep. It was his job to make sure that no wolves came to hurt them. But the boy grew tired of having no one but sheep to talk to.

One day, he wanted excitement so badly that he raised his voice and sang out as loud as he could, "Wolf! Wolf! There's a wolf chasing our sheep!"

His voice carried all the way to town. When the villagers heard him, they stopped what they were doing and ran as fast as they could to the top of the hill.

"Where is the wolf?" they cried. "Has it hurt our sheep?"

The shepherd boy just laughed in their faces, "I fooled you, I fooled you. There is no wolf!"

"Don't cry wolf when there is no wolf, child!" said the villagers. "We have work to do!"

But the boy just **grinned** at them.

A few days later, the boy felt restless again. He decided to play the same trick.

"Wolf! Wolf!" he cried. Once again, the villagers left their work and ran to the top of the hill.

When they saw that there was no wolf they sternly said, "Child, do not waste our time like this. It is dangerous to cry wolf when there is no wolf."

The boy did not know what they meant. He laughed even harder this time, proud that he had been able to fool the grownups twice.

A few days later, a wolf really did come out of the forest. It snuck up close to the sheep and the boy was very frightened.

"Wolf! Wolf!" he cried out. "A wolf has come to get our sheep!"

But when the people in the village heard the shepherd boy, they assumed he was fooling them again. So they kept on doing their work and did not go to him.

Soon, the **entire** flock was scattered. The boy was in tears as he climbed down the hill.

When the villagers found out what happened, they shook their heads. "We told you it was dangerous to lie," said an old man.

"A liar will not be believed even when he tells the truth," said an old woman.

The villagers set out to find the sheep and the boy promised to never cry wolf again!

Listening Comprehension

What do you think the villagers mean when they tell the boy it is dangerous to cry wolf when there is no wolf?

WONDERFUL WORD

entire

Define: *Entire* means all or whole.
Example: The hungry cat ate the *entire* can of food.
Ask: What do you do with your *entire* class? What do you do in a small group?

Respond to the Story

Retell: Use the prompts on the back of the Retelling Cards to help children retell the story.

Think About It

1. What do you think the boy learned about crying wolf?

2. How do you think this story could help you in your life?

Activity: Talk to children about when they would call for help. Have children create signs that they could wave in the air if they needed help. Reread the story. Have them hold up their signs the last time the boy calls "Wolf!"

The Bremen Town Musicians

A Tale from Germany

WONDERFUL WORD

weak

Define: *Weak* means not strong or powerful.
Example: Kim felt very *weak* after she was sick.
Ask: What are some things that a *weak* person can do to become stronger?

Listening Comprehension

Why does the donkey run away? Why do the other animals run away? What do they have in common?

Once there was a donkey who had worked hard for many, many years. But he was growing old and tired, and could no longer pull heavy loads. "There's no work here for an old donkey," said his master.

So the donkey ran away. He set off directly for Bremen Town. "There," he thought, "I will be a musician."

On his way, the donkey found a hound lying on the road, gasping as if he had just run for days. "Why are you gasping like that?" asked the donkey.

"Ah," replied the hound, "I am now old and too **weak** to hunt. My master no longer wanted me, so I ran away. But how will I find food to fill my hungry belly?"

"I am going to Bremen Town, and shall be a musician there," said the donkey. "Come with me and you, too, can be a musician."

The hound agreed, and on they went.

Before long, they came to a cat that was sitting on the path, crying. "What has gone wrong with you?" asked the donkey.

"I am old now," answered the cat, "and I prefer to sit by the fire and rest, rather than run outside all day. My mistress said I'm always underfoot, and sent me away. But where will I go?"

"Go with us to Bremen Town," said the donkey. "You, too, can be a musician."

The cat liked the idea, and went with them.

Soon after, the three travelers walked by a farm where a rooster was crowing with all his might. "What is the matter?" asked the donkey.

"My mistress has told the cook that she intends to eat me in the soup tomorrow," said the rooster. "Now I am crowing as loudly as I can, for I will never crow again."

"Come with us," said the donkey. "We are going to Bremen Town. You have a good voice, and will help us **perform** as musicians!"

The rooster agreed to this plan, and all four went on together.

By evening, all of the animals were very hungry. They came to a small house deep inside the forest. The house belonged to a band of robbers. The donkey looked inside the window.

"I see a table covered with good things to eat and drink," said the donkey. "And three robbers are having a feast!"

WONDERFUL WORD

perform

Define: To *perform* is to give a show in public.
Example: A singer will *perform* at the party.
Ask: Have you ever seen anyone *perform*? What did they do?

"If they are robbers, then I see no reason why we should not share in the feast," said the rooster.

"Yes, yes," agreed the hound and the cat.

The animals thought of a plan to drive away the robbers. This is what they did. The donkey placed his front feet on the window ledge. The hound jumped on the donkey's back. The cat climbed upon the hound, and the rooster flew up and perched upon the head of the cat.

Then the animals began to perform their music together. The donkey brayed. The hound barked. The cat meowed. And the rooster crowed. The animals burst through the window, shattering the glass.

At this horrible noise, the robbers jumped up and ran out into the forest in a great fright.

Then the four animal companions sat down at the table and happily ate from all of the good foods that were left.

After the meal each animal found a place to sleep. The donkey laid down in the yard, the hound slept behind the door, the cat curled up near the warm ashes of the fire, and the rooster perched on the roof.

Later, when the robbers saw that all was quiet, one of them went back to **examine** the house.

Inside, the robber saw the glistening, fiery eyes of the cat, which he thought were bright coals burning in the fireplace. He leaned down to warm himself, but the cat flew in his face, spitting and scratching. "What's that?" cried the robber. He was very frightened, and ran to the door, but the hound sprang up and bit his leg. Then the robber ran across the yard, where the donkey gave him a kick with its hind foot. "Oh no!" the robber yelled.

As it was dark, and the robber could not see, he thought that he had been scratched, bitten, and kicked by a terrible monster.

Then the rooster woke up from all the noise and cried down from the roof, "Cock-a-doodle-doo!" The robber was sure he'd heard the monster say, "Catch a robber, too!"

"Help! Help!" the robber cried as he ran back to his friends. When he told them about the terrible monster that had taken over their house, they all quickly ran away, never to return.

The house suited the four musicians of Bremen Town so well that they decided to stay and make it their home.

WONDERFUL WORD

examine
Define: *Examine* means check out or look over.
Example: After I dropped the bowl, I *examined* it to see if it was broken.
Ask: Why does the doctor need to *examine* you when you're sick?

Listening Comprehension

What happens to the robber who goes back to the house?

Respond to the Story

Retell: Use the prompts on the back of the Retelling Cards to help children retell the story.

Think About It

1. Why were the robbers so frightened by the animals?

2. Where were the animals originally going? Why didn't they get there?

Activity: Have children draw their favorite characters from the story. Help them to cut out the characters and glue them to flat sticks, to make puppets. Children can use their puppets to act out the story. Encourage them to talk in voices their characters would use.

The Bremen Town Musicians **19**

Brer Rabbit Meets Brer Lion

An African American Tale

WONDERFUL WORD

announcement

Define: To make an *announcement* is to tell news to everyone.

Example: Pedro made an *announcement* about his new baby brother.

Ask: What would you make an *announcement* about?

Listening Comprehension

How do you think Brer Rabbit feels when Brer Lion comes to the neighborhood?

Brer Rabbit may not have been the biggest animal around, but many thought he was the smartest. Some animals liked him. Others spent their waking hours figuring how to get back at him for his tricky ways. But there was one thing you had to say about Brer Rabbit. He had big brains. Animals paid attention to him, and some even thought he was the boss.

Then Brer Lion came to the neighborhood. Now, Brer Lion was so big and so loud and so mean that all of the animals just naturally listened to him right away. But that wasn't good enough for Brer Lion. He wanted to be boss. So one day, he made a big **announcement**. He said that he was going to eat one member of every animal family around.

Well, the animals all started crying and moaning when they heard about that. Naturally, Brer Rabbit didn't want to get eaten. And try as he may, he couldn't make himself at all comfortable with the idea of a member of his family getting eaten either. He passed the time planning and scheming.

When it came time for Brer Lion to eat a rabbit, Brer Rabbit decided to go have a talk with Brer Lion. Anything beat sitting around and waiting.

"I'll be home in time for dinner," Brer Rabbit told his wife and children. They started crying like they were just born two days ago because they knew for sure that Brer Lion would eat him. But Brer Rabbit told them to quit worrying; there was no way he was going to miss his dinner.

On the way to Brer Lion's, Brer Rabbit was planning and scheming. When he came to the river, he bent over to see his reflection in the water. He put a little mud on his face and mussed up his hair. He undid his buttons and then buttoned them up the wrong way. Then he sucked in his tummy to make himself look even skinnier than he was and went on his way.

He rang Brer Lion's bell. When Brer Lion came to the door, he looked at Brer Rabbit up, down, and sideways.

"There's not a lot that looks worth eating on you," Brer Lion observed at last.

"Maybe so," replied Brer Rabbit. "I sure wish I could be a better meal for you, Brer Lion. I know I'm not fat and I have a few fleas on me and its been a year since I've had a bath so maybe I smell a bit. But I'm here to be eaten. So let's get on with it."

Listening Comprehension

Why do you think Brer Rabbit puts mud on himself and tries to make himself look skinny?

satisfying
Define: *Satisfying* means having enough or having what you want.
Example: Lisa thinks two slices of pizza is a *satisfying* amount.
Ask: How many slices of pizza do you find *satisfying*?

Brer Lion looked at Brer Rabbit and shook his head in disgust. "You're so puny that I'm going to have to eat your entire family to get one **satisfying** meal," he said.

"Maybe so, Brer Lion," said Brer Rabbit. "I sure wish I was as fat and healthy as the creature I just saw at the river on my way here. I said to myself, 'I wish I was that juicy so Brer Lion could have a feast on me.'"

"What creature is that, Brer Rabbit?" asked Brer Lion.

"I didn't ask his name," answered Brer Rabbit. "My mind was too full with the idea of being your dinner in a few minutes. But he sure looked tasty."

"Bring me to him," said Brer Lion.

Brer Rabbit let his head hang low. "That creature is too big and fierce looking, Brer Lion. I'm afraid of what might happen to you if you were to meet up with him."

That got Brer Lion mad. "There's no creature too big and fierce for me, Brer Rabbit. BRING ME TO HIM!" he roared.

So Brer Rabbit brought Brer Lion to the river. He looked into the water. "That creature was around here somewhere, Brer Lion," he said.

Brer Lion walked up and looked in the water himself. And sure enough, he saw a big creature with a long mane looking back at him.

Brer Lion roared. And sure enough, the creature in the river roared back. Brer Lion showed his teeth. And sure enough, the creature in the river showed his teeth. Then Brer Lion got so mad he jumped in the river headfirst.

Now Brer Lion might have been the biggest and fiercest animal around but he didn't know the first thing about swimming. He was thrashing around headed downstream when Brer Rabbit waved good-bye. Brer Lion knew better than to come back that way again.

That night all the animals celebrated. Even Brer Lion was no match for Brer Rabbit's big brains. And nobody was more **pleased** about it than Brer Rabbit himself.

Listening Comprehension

Why does Brer Rabbit tell Brer Lion that the creature is too big and fierce for him?

WONDERFUL WORD

pleased

Define: *Pleased* means felt happy about.
Example: Brittany was *pleased* that her mom liked the birthday present.
Ask: What makes you feel *pleased* at school?

Respond to the Story

Retell: Use the prompts on the back of the Retelling Cards to help children retell the story.

Think About It

1. How did Brer Rabbit trick Brer Lion? Who was the creature in the river?

2. How would you describe Brer Rabbit? What is he like?

Activity: Help children explore their own reflections by making faces in a mirror. Have them name the feeling that goes with each face. Have them draw one of their faces and dictate the feeling word that describes it.

Cinderella

A Tale from France

WONDERFUL WORD

cruel

Define: *Cruel* means very mean.

Example: I don't like to play with children who are *cruel*.

Ask: Can you name other story characters who are *cruel*?

Listening Comprehension

What is Cinderella like? How is she different from her stepsisters?

Once there was a young girl named Ella. After Ella's mother died, her father married again, and his new wife became Ella's stepmother. This new wife was proud and **cruel**, and she had two daughters who were exactly like her.

Almost as soon as the wedding took place, Ella's new stepmother and stepsisters began to make her life a misery.

"What is this useless creature doing in our good rooms?" her stepmother said. "Away to the kitchen with her! If she wants to eat, then she must work for her food. She will be our servant."

Ella's stepsisters took all of her dresses away from her and gave her rags to wear. "These are good enough for you!" they said.

Then they put her to work. Poor Ella got up every day before sunrise, carried water, made the fire, cooked, served, and washed. She only had a few leftovers to eat. She had no bed to sleep in so she slept near the fireplace to keep warm. Because of this she was often covered in ashes–or cinders–so everyone started to call her Cinderella.

Even in her ragged clothing with ashes on her face, Cinderella was a hundred times more beautiful than her stepsisters. And she was as good and kind as she was beautiful.

One day, news arrived that the king was going to have a ball. At this ball his son, the prince, would choose a bride. The two proud stepsisters were invited. Immediately, they started to prepare for it. It was Cinderella's job to help.

"I think the prince will like me in this the best," said the older stepsister, trying on a red gown.

"This necklace is exactly the color of my eyes," said the younger stepsister.

"Don't you wish you could go to the ball, Cinderella?" they teased. Then they laughed. For everyone knew that Cinderella, covered in rags and ashes, would never be invited to the king's ball.

At last, the evening of the ball came and Cinderella watched her stepsisters leave in their coach. When she lost sight of them, she began to **weep**.

Her godmother, who was a fairy, appeared just then. "What is wrong, child?" she asked.

"I wish I could . . . I wish I could . . ." Cinderella was crying so much that she could not finish.

"I know, my dear," said her fairy godmother. "You wish you could go to the ball." Cinderella nodded.

"Well, then you shall," said her godmother. "First, go to the pumpkin patch and fetch me the best pumpkin you can find."

Cinderella soon returned with a pumpkin. Her fairy godmother touched it with her magic wand and it turned into a beautiful coach. Next, her godmother called softly into a mouse hole and six little mice came out. As she tapped them one by one with her wand, they turned into stately gray horses to draw the coach. Then a stray cat came by. The fairy godmother quickly tapped it with her wand. Before Cinderella's eyes, the cat became a coachman with a long beard, to drive the coach.

"I hope your coach pleases you, my dear," said her godmother.

"Oh, yes!" answered Cinderella. "But how can I go to the ball wearing these rags?"

Her godmother simply touched Cinderella with her wand and at once her clothes were turned into a gown of gold and silver. Then she gave Cinderella the most beautiful glass slippers.

Just as Cinderella was about to leave, her fairy godmother said, "Be sure to be back by midnight, my dear. If you stay even a minute longer, then your coach will turn back into a pumpkin, your horses will be mice, and your coachman will be a cat. And your gown will once again be rags."

WONDERFUL WORD

weep
Define: To *weep* is to cry.
Example: When the baby misses his mommy, he *weeps*.
Ask: How do people feel when they *weep*?

Listening Comprehension

Who is the fairy godmother? How does she help Cinderella?

Listening Comprehension

Does Cinderella want to leave the ball? Why does she run away?

WONDERFUL WORD

vanished

Define: *Vanished* means disappeared or no longer able to be seen.

Example: The magician waved his wand and the rabbit *vanished*.

Ask: Why do some cats *vanish* when they see dogs?

Cinderella promised. Then she was off. The magic coach flew through the air to the palace. The prince had been told that a great princess would soon arrive, and he ran out to receive Cinderella himself. He led her into the hall. A hush came over the guests as they entered.

"How lovely she is!" everyone whispered.

The prince led her across the floor and they danced together again and again. A fine meal was served but the young prince only gazed at Cinderella, and could not eat a bite. After the meal, they danced some more, and as they danced they spoke of everything. Cinderella was so happy that she forgot to watch the clock and suddenly it struck twelve midnight.

At once, she dashed away. Though the prince rushed after her, he could not catch her. In her haste, she left behind one of the glass slippers, which he picked up and carried with him.

Cinderella's coach had **vanished** and she had to run home in the dark. Her fine clothes were gone, too. All that remained was the other glass slipper, which Cinderella had taken off to hold as she ran.

When her stepsisters came home, they talked and talked about the mysterious princess from the ball. "Of course, one so low as you, Cinderella, could barely imagine her loveliness," they said.

A few days later, the king announced that his son would marry the young woman who had left her glass slipper at the ball. The prince was determined to find the mysterious princess, and he knew that only she could fit her foot perfectly into the glass slipper. The prince's men went from house to house, trying the slipper on every young woman in the land.

Time went by, but nowhere could they find a woman whose foot fit into the slipper. At last, it was brought to the two stepsisters. They each pushed and pushed, trying to squeeze a foot inside. But they could not.

Cinderella said, "Let me try it on."

Her sisters began to laugh and tease her. But the prince's men looked at Cinderella and saw her kindness and beauty. They offered her the slipper, and it went on her foot at once. Then, while her stepsisters watched in astonishment, Cinderella drew from her pocket the other glass slipper and put it on too.

Now the stepsisters knew that Cinderella had been the princess they had admired at the ball! They threw themselves at her feet to beg her forgiveness. Cinderella hugged them and said that she forgave them with all her heart.

Then Cinderella was taken to the prince. He was overwhelmed with love for her and soon they were married. They were happy together from that day forth.

Listening Comprehension

Is looking for the girl who fits in the glass slipper a good way to find Cinderella? Why or why not?

Respond to the Story

Retell: Use the prompts on the back of the Retelling Cards to help children retell the story.

Think About It

1. Why do you think the stepsisters treated Cinderella so badly?

2. Why did the prince want to marry Cinderella? Why did she want to marry him?

Activity: Invite each child to pretend that they have their own fairy godmother. Have each child draw a picture of her and dictate a sentence telling how she would help them.

City Mouse and Country Mouse

A Fable by Aesop

WONDERFUL WORD

stored

Define: *Stored* means put away to use later.
Example: After we did the shopping, we *stored* all of the food in the pantry.
Ask: Where do you put things that need to be *stored*?

Listening Comprehension

Why does City Mouse call Country Mouse "you poor thing"?

There was once a happy little Country Mouse who lived in a big wheat field. In the summer, she feasted on grains of wheat or bits of bread from the farmers' lunch boxes. When the weather grew cold, she moved into the farmhouse and picked up bits of cake and bread and cheese that the cook dropped on the kitchen floor. These she **stored** away in her little mouse hole in the attic until she had a good supply for the winter.

One winter day, Country Mouse's cousin, City Mouse, came to visit. Country Mouse took City Mouse to see her attic pantry. Proudly, she showed him the mound of cheese bits, the heaps of bread and cake crumbs, and the neat piles of nuts and dried peas.

But after City Mouse had eaten a hearty dinner, he wiped his whiskers and said, "You poor thing! So this is the way you live, on dried up leftovers. Come with me to the city and I will show you a real feast!"

Country Mouse immediately felt ashamed of her simple home. She wanted to see if her cousin's city life was as grand as he said, so she went with him to the city.

City Mouse led the way into a huge brick house, up a great staircase, and into a dining room.

The rich people who lived in the big house were just having dinner, so the two little mice hid behind the door.

"Keep very still," said City Mouse. "When they leave the table, we can have all the food that is left."

The eyes of little Country Mouse grew big and round, for she had never seen so much food in her whole life. She stood very still. Then she heard feet scuffling and chairs scraping as the big people left the table.

"Come on," squeaked City Mouse. Peeking **cautiously** right and left, he led the way across the room. He hopped onto a chair, and from the chair onto the table. Country Mouse scampered along behind him.

Country Mouse took a long look around her at the table still crowded with good things, and sighed a deep, happy sigh.

"This is wonderful," she said, taking a big bite of cheese. "You live just like a prince!"

She had scarcely finished speaking when a snarling cat pounced onto the table. Then the cook ran into the room, shouting and waving a big spoon. Then two dogs came in, barking fiercely. Then there was a terrible ruckus! In the midst of it, the two mice skittered down to the floor and dodged into a handy hole.

WONDERFUL WORD

cautiously
Define: *Cautiously* means carefully.
Example: Justin climbed the tree slowly and *cautiously*.
Ask: When have you acted *cautiously*? What did you do?

Listening Comprehension

Why do the mice need to be more careful in the city?

prefer

Define: To *prefer* is to like some things better than other things.

Example: I like watching movies, but I *prefer* listening to stories.

Ask: Which do you *prefer*, playing at home or at the park?

Listening Comprehension

Why does Country Mouse want to go back home? Do you think she made the right decision?

"We'll wait until all is quiet again and go back for some more," whispered City Mouse.

But his country cousin shook her head firmly.

"We'll wait until it is quiet again and then I'll go home as fast as I can. You are welcome to all the fine food you can get, my friend. As for me, I **prefer** my dry crusts in my peaceful attic!"

Respond to the Story

Retell: Use the prompts on the back of the Retelling Cards to help children retell the story.

Think About It

1. How is the country different from the city? What things do you find in each place?

2. City Mouse thinks that his life is better than his cousin's. After visiting the city, what does Country Mouse think? Whose life do you think is better?

Activity: Help children to compare life in the city and in the country. Have them look for pictures in magazines and books that show city life and country life. As a group, list things you might see or do in the city and in the country.

The Clever Jackal

A Tale from India

A poor man was walking home through the forest when he came upon a tiger who was standing in a deep hole.

"Oh my," said the man. "What happened to you?"

"I was walking just as you are now," said the tiger, "when I fell into this hole. And here I have sat for many days growing hungrier and thirstier. If you don't help me get out, I will surely die."

Now the poor man was very kindhearted and could not bear to see a fellow being in trouble. But he was also aware that tigers had a reputation for eating people.

"If I let you out, how do I know that you won't eat me?" asked the man.

"Do you think that I would be so ungrateful as to eat the one who sets me free?" asked the tiger. "I give you my promise. I will not **harm** you."

So the man decided to help the tiger. He found a log. The tiger grabbed it. Soon, he was out of the hole.

"Now," said the tiger to the man, "it is time for me to eat you!"

"Eat me?" cried the man. "But you promised!"

Listening Comprehension

Do you think the man should help the tiger get out of the hole? Why or why not?

WONDERFUL WORD

harm

Define: *Harm* means to hurt.

Example: Leaving toys out in the rain might *harm* them.

Ask: How can we try not to *harm* small animals?

fair
Define: *Fair* means to get what seems right or deserved.
Example: It seemed *fair* that the children who helped out got to eat first.
Ask: What is a *fair* way to divide a pizza among six children?

Listening Comprehension

Do you think it's fair that the tiger eat the man? Why or why not?

"What do I care for a silly promise?" asked the tiger. "I haven't had a meal for many days and you look so tasty!"

"Wait!" said the man. "This is not fair! If it weren't for me, you would still be stuck in that hole."

"The world is not a **fair** place," said the tiger. "Everyone knows that."

"That doesn't mean you should eat me," said the man.

"The whole world agrees with me," said the tiger. "Ask that tree over there and it will tell you."

The man went up to the tree. "Good day, Tree," he began. "I rescued this tiger from a hole and now he wants to eat me. Do you think that is fair?"

"Fair?" asked the tree. "The world is not a fair place. Look at me. I give cooling shade to everyone who passes by. But what do I get for my troubles? People cut off my branches to build their houses and make their fires. I think it's fine for the tiger to eat you."

"I told you," the tiger said to the man. "Prepare to be eaten."

"Wait!" begged the man. "Let us just ask this road beneath our feet."

"Very well," said the tiger.

"Good day, Road," said the man. "I rescued this tiger from a hole and now he wants to eat me. Do you think that is fair?"

"The world is not a fair place," said the road. "Look at me. I help everyone get where they want to go. But what do I get for my troubles? People wear me down with their footsteps and throw their trash on me. I think it's fine for the tiger to eat you."

"I told you," said the tiger. "Prepare to be eaten."

Just then a jackal came by.

"Please," said the man. "Let us ask this jackal. We will do as she says."

"Very well," said the tiger, who had decided to eat the man no matter what.

"Jackal," said the man. "Today I rescued this tiger and now he plans to eat me. Do you think that is fair?"

The jackal rubbed her head. "I don't understand what you are saying. Can you explain it again?"

The man repeated himself.

"I still don't understand what you are saying," said the jackal. "I don't know what's wrong with me today."

The tiger was beginning to get **impatient**. He explained the situation to the jackal again.

"I'm still not getting it," said the jackal. "I think you will have to show me. Where did it all begin?"

The tiger and the man brought the jackal to the hole in the ground. Then the tiger told the whole story.

"Oh dear," said the jackal. "I am as confused as ever. Where did it all begin?"

"I was IN the hole, you foolish beast," shouted the tiger. "I was IN the hole!"

"What do you mean you were in the hole?" asked the jackal. "Can you show me?"

"Show you? Of course, I can show you!" said the tiger. And he jumped back in the hole.

Listening Comprehension

How would you describe the tiger? What is his personality like?

WONDERFUL WORD

impatient
Define: Someone who is *impatient* can't wait or doesn't want to wait.
Example: I got *impatient* waiting for the bus.
Ask: When do you feel *impatient*?

"Now do you understand me?" he shouted from the bottom of the hole.

"I understand you perfectly well," said the jackal. "You started out in the hole and there you shall stay."

"Come," she said to the man. "Let us get away from this ungrateful creature."

"Thank you!" said the man. "The world may not always be a fair place but good friends like you help to make it better."

"I understand that perfectly," said the jackal.

Respond to the Story

Retell: Use the prompts on the back of the Retelling Cards to help children retell the story.

Think About It

1. How did the jackal help the man? Do you think the tiger was surprised by what happened? Why or why not?

2. How would you describe the tiger? What lesson do you think the tiger learned?

Activity: Talk about whether the tiger acted fairly or not. Invite children to draw the tiger and the man. The tiger can either be acting fairly toward the man by thanking him or unfairly by threatening to eat him. Have children dictate speech balloons with the tiger's words.

The Crocodile and the Hen

A Tale from Central Africa

Once there was a hen who went to the river to have a drink of water and look for a bit of food. As the hen was sipping water, a crocodile came up to her.

"How tasty you look!" said the crocodile. "I am going to eat you!"

The hen answered, "Oh, please do not eat me, my dear brother!"

The crocodile was so surprised by what the hen said that he went away. "How can I be the hen's brother?" he thought. "She lives on land, and I live in the water. We are not alike at all!"

The next day, the hen was at the river again, looking for food.

When the crocodile saw her, he said, "You look even more delicious today. I regret to say that I must eat you."

The hen answered, "Oh, please do not eat me, dear brother. We have so much **in common**, you and I." Then she gave the crocodile her most pleasant smile.

The crocodile was so confused that he skulked away. "I must consider what the hen said," he thought. "If I am the hen's brother, then the hen is my sister. But how can that be? She lives on land, and I live in the water. We are not alike at all!"

On the third day, the hen was at the river once again, drinking water. When the crocodile saw her, he could not believe that he had let her get away from him twice.

"This is getting ridiculous!" he said. "You have tricked me out of eating you for two whole days now. But I will not let your sly ways keep me from eating you today."

WONDERFUL WORD

in common

Define: *In common* means shared.

Example: Jon and Carolina both love dinosaurs. They have something *in common*.

Ask: What do you have *in common* with the other children in your class?

Listening Comprehension

Is the hen afraid of the crocodile? How do you know?

Listening Comprehension

Why do you think the hen calls the crocodile her brother?

WONDERFUL WORD

correct

Define: *Correct* means true or right.

Example: When you send a letter, make sure you write the *correct* address on the envelope.

Ask: What do you do if someone asks you a question and you don't know the *correct* answer?

The hen answered, "Please do not eat me, dear brother. Perhaps we can talk for a while and enjoy each other's company."

But this time, the crocodile was very, very annoyed with the hen.

He said angrily, "Hen, I am *not* your brother! In fact, I do not even think we are cousins!" Then he stomped off.

The next day, the crocodile went to visit his best friend, a lizard. "Hello, dear friend," said the crocodile. "I have a problem, and I hope you can help me. Each day, a hen comes to the river and, when I get ready to eat her, she says that I am her brother! How can that be?"

"The hen is **correct**, dear brother," said the lizard. "Don't you know that the hen is a bird? And the bird, the turtle, the lizard, and the crocodile all lay eggs. That makes all of us brothers and sisters!"

The crocodile thought and thought and then a big smile came to his face.

"What you say is true!" he said. "Thank you so much for helping me to understand."

And that is why, to this day, a crocodile will never, ever eat a hen!

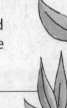

Respond to the Story

Retell: Use the prompts on the back of the Retelling Cards to help children retell the story.

Think About It

1. How are the hen and the crocodile alike? How are they different?

2. Do you think the crocodile might want to eat the lizard? Why or why not?

Activity: Have children choose two animals and draw a picture of each. Then have them describe what the two animals have in common.

The Foolish, Timid Rabbit

A Tale from India

Once upon a time, there lived a foolish and **timid** rabbit. One day, the rabbit was resting under a palm tree. Suddenly, he thought, "What if the earth should break up into little pieces? What would happen to me?"

Now at that same moment, a little monkey dropped a big coconut from high up in the tree. It fell to the ground right behind the rabbit and made a loud noise.

The rabbit jumped. "Oh goodness!" he cried. "It is happening! The earth is breaking up!" And he ran off as fast as he could, without even looking back to see what made the noise.

Another rabbit saw him running, and called out, "Why are you running so quickly?"

The first rabbit answered, "Dear rabbit, beware! The earth is breaking up!" And so the second rabbit ran along with him. As they ran, one rabbit after another joined them until there were many, many rabbits running as fast as they could.

The rabbits ran past a deer. "The earth is breaking up!" they cried. So the deer ran along with them.

The deer saw a fox on the way and shouted out that the earth was breaking up. So the fox joined them. They passed an elephant. The fox told the elephant that the earth was breaking up, and she joined them, too.

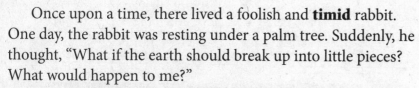

wise

Define: *Wise* means smart and having good judgment.
Example: The *wise* woman always knew what to do.
Ask: Who do you think is *wise*? What makes this person *wise*?

Listening Comprehension

Why are all of the animals running? What else could they have done when the rabbit told them the news?

At last, the **wise** lion saw the animals running, and heard their fearful cries.

The lion roared three times. The animals stopped in their tracks, for the lion was the king of the animals.

"Why are you running so fast?" asked the lion.

"Oh, King Lion," they replied, "don't you know that the earth is breaking up?"

The lion thought there must be some mistake. So he asked, "Who saw the earth breaking up?"

"I didn't," said the elephant. "The fox told me about it."

"I didn't," said the fox. "The deer told me about it."

"I didn't," said the deer. "The rabbits told me about it."

Then one after another, the rabbits said, "I didn't see it, but another rabbit told me about it."

After asking many questions, the lion finally came to the rabbit who had first said that the earth was breaking up.

"Why do you think the earth is breaking up?" the lion asked the rabbit.

"Well," said the rabbit, "I was sitting under a palm tree. Then I **wondered**, 'What would happen to me if the earth were to break up?' After that I heard a loud sound, and I knew it was happening! So I ran away!"

"We must go back to the place where this happened to find out what is going on," said the lion. So he put the rabbit on his back and ran like the wind to find the place where the whole thing had started. The other animals waited.

When they found the tree, the lion pointed to the coconut on the ground. He said, "Foolish rabbit, the sound you heard was this coconut falling!"

Then the lion ran back to the other animals, and told about the coconut. And everyone was happy that the earth was not breaking up!

Respond to the Story

Retell: Use the prompts on the back of the Retelling Cards to help children retell the story.

Think About It

1. What do you think the little rabbit learned by the end of the story? What do you think the other animals learned?

2. Why is it important to not always believe what someone tells you?

Activity: A coconut falling from a palm tree was what scared the rabbit. Have children cut out trees from magazines and paste them onto a tree collage. Talk about the trees and what might fall from them. Create a new version of the story using a different kind of tree.

Grandmother Spider Brings the Sun

A Cherokee Tale

A long time ago, when the world was still new, the animals had no heat or light. When they walked, they bumped into each other in the darkness. When they sat still, they could hardly stop **shivering** from the cold. Something needed to be done. So they held a meeting.

"We animals need heat and light," said Coyote. His teeth chattered as he spoke.

All the animals stomped their feet in agreement.

Jackal stepped forward. "I have heard of something that gives off heat and light. It is called the sun. It lives over on the other side of the world."

Owl spoke from the top of a tree. "I have heard of it too," he said. "It is big and strong and has enough heat and light for all animals. But it's such a long way away. How will we ever get there?"

"And even if we do get there, how could we carry back something so hot without getting burned?" wondered Tortoise.

The animals started talking loudly about how they could bring back the sun.

Then a voice rang out above the others, "Let me do it!" The voice belonged to Possum. "My tail is bushy and full," he said. "I can take a little bit of the sun and put it in my tail and I won't even feel it."

So Possum went off to find the sun. As he got closer, the sun got hotter and brighter. He had to shade his eyes. But he kept going. When he finally got there, he grabbed a little piece of the sun and put it in his tail. He started home. But soon the sun got so hot that it burned off all the fur from his tail, and he dropped it. This is why, to this day, possums have bare tails.

The animals still did not have heat or light. They held another meeting.

"I will go!" came a bold voice. It was Eagle. "I am strong and fast. I can bring the sun back before it begins to burn."

So Eagle flew all the way to the sun. Then he dove down to **grab** a piece of it. He put it on top of his head and with his mighty wings flew off. But even Eagle wasn't fast enough. Soon, the sun began to burn the top of his head and he had to shake it off. This is why, to this day, many eagles have bald heads.

The animals still did not have heat or light. So they held another meeting.

"If mighty Eagle cannot get the sun, who among us can?" asked Jackal.

"Perhaps a very small creature could do it," came a tiny voice.

"Who is that speaking?" the animals asked.

"It is I, Grandmother Spider," said the tiny voice. "I have a way to bring the sun's heat and light to you."

The animals laughed. If great Eagle could not bring the sun, then how could a little spider, no bigger than the tip of one of Eagle's huge talons, ever succeed?

But Grandmother Spider was very clever. She had already started making a tiny clay pot with her nimble legs. When she finished the pot, she hung it from one of her threads and then spun a web that reached all the way to the sun.

WONDERFUL WORD

grab

Define: To *grab* is to take quickly.
Example: Everyone can *grab* a gift bag at the end of the party.
Ask: What things do you *grab* from home before you leave for school?

Listening Comprehension

What problems do Possum and Eagle have when they try to get the sun?

Listening Comprehension

Why don't the other animals want Grandmother Spider to go? How do you feel about their reason?

WONDERFUL WORD

accomplish
Define: *Accomplish* means get done.
Example: We have a lot of work to *accomplish* today.
Ask: What did you *accomplish* in school yesterday?

When she got there, she snatched a tiny bit of the sun and put it in the clay pot. She climbed back down the web with the pot dangling from one of her threads.

As she traveled, the sun's light and warmth shone out and the world got lighter and warmer with every step she took. The animals rejoiced.

"All praise Grandmother Spider!" they cried. Never again did they question what a small animal could **accomplish**.

And that is how the animals first got heat and light.

Respond to the Story

Retell: Use the prompts on the back of the Retelling Cards to help children retell the story.

Think About It

1. What do you think the world would be like if there were no sun?

2. Explain why Grandmother Spider's plan was so clever. What did she do that Possum and Eagle didn't?

Activity: Invite children to make their own 3-dimensional pictures of Grandmother Spider bringing the sun. Have them collage yellow and red tissue paper for the sun. Then have them use yarn and glue to create a web on the sun. They can add Grandmother Spider after the web has dried.

Jack and the Beanstalk

A Tale from England

Once upon a time there was a boy named Jack who lived in a tiny house with his mother. They were very poor. One day, Jack's mother said, "Our old cow **refuses** to give us milk. Take her to the market and sell her. And be sure to fetch a good price!"

Jack was walking to the market with the old cow at his side when he met a funny-looking old man. The man said, "I see you're off to sell that old cow. I'd like to buy her. I'll pay you with these beans here in my hand."

"Beans!" cried Jack. "I cannot sell our cow for a few beans!"

"Ah, but these are very special beans," said the man. "If you plant them at night, by morning the stalks will be right up to the sky."

"Really?" asked Jack. He was very curious to see if it were true, so he took the beans and gave up the old cow.

When Jack got home and told his mother just what he had done, she said, "You sold our precious cow for a handful of beans? I never knew my son was such a fool!" She tossed the beans out the window, and sent Jack to bed without supper.

In the morning, Jack looked out his little window and was amazed to see an enormous beanstalk, thick as a tree. The old man had told the truth! The beanstalk reached all the way up into the clouds.

Jack grabbed hold of the stalk and began climbing. He climbed and climbed until at last he reached the sky.

WONDERFUL WORD

refuses

Define: *Refuses* means will not do something.
Example: Benjamin *refuses* to eat zucchini.
Ask: What is something that you sometimes *refuse* to do?

Listening Comprehension

How does Jack's mother feel when Jack comes home and tells her what he did?

Jack saw a great, big, tall house. The door was open so he walked right in. Though Jack was a good-sized boy, inside this house he felt like a mouse. The chairs and tables were high above his head. Suddenly, he heard a sound like an earthquake, and quickly hid himself. BOOM, BOOM, BOOM, shook the floor. Two giants came in the room, a man and a woman each as tall as a tree.

The two sat down for breakfast. Suddenly, the giant man sniffed the air and said,

**Fee-fum-fo-fi,
Someone's come into the sky!**

"**Nonsense**, dear," said his wife. "It's just us here. Let's go take our nap." And with that, the two got up and left.

Jack tiptoed out of the kitchen to see where the giants had gone. He found the two snoring on two enormous sofas. The man had several bags of gold under his arms and a few at his feet. Very quietly and slowly, Jack took one of those bags of gold and made his way back to the beanstalk. Then he climbed down until at last he got home.

"Well, mother, wasn't I right about the beans?" said Jack as he showed her the bag of gold.

They lived on the bag of gold for some time, but at last they came to the end of it, and Jack made up his mind to once more climb to the top of the beanstalk.

So one morning, he got up early and he climbed and climbed until at last he reached the sky, and the great, big, tall house of the giants.

Jack crawled into the living room and hid behind a curtain. The giant man was lying on the sofa, and his wife was coming into the room.

Listening Comprehension

Why does Jack feel like a mouse in the giants' house?

WONDERFUL WORD

nonsense

Define: *Nonsense* means something that is silly or ridiculous.
Example: It is *nonsense* to ask a dog to help you read a book.
Ask: What is the silliest piece of *nonsense* you've ever heard?

"Here's the hen that lays the golden eggs," she said. The giant said, "Lay!" and the hen laid an egg of gold. Suddenly, the giant sniffed the air, and said,

Fee-fum-fo-fi,
Someone's here with you and I!

"Nonsense, dear," said his wife. "You're dreaming again. You must need a nap."

The giant then began to snore, and his wife left the room, so Jack caught hold of the golden hen, and was off in an instant. He climbed down the beanstalk as fast as he could. When he got home, he showed his mother the wonderful hen. Each time Jack said "Lay!" the hen laid a golden egg.

Well, Jack was not content, and it wasn't long before he decided to try his luck at the top of the beanstalk once again. So one morning, he got up early and he climbed and climbed, until at last he reached the sky, and the great, big, tall house of the giants.

Inside the house, the giants were resting in the library. There was a golden harp on the table. The giant's wife said, "Sing!" and the golden harp sang most beautifully. Soon, the two giants were snoring. Jack crawled along the floor until he was right at the giants' feet. He caught hold of the golden harp and dashed with it toward the door.

But the harp called out quite loudly, "Master, Mistress!" and the giants woke up just in time to see Jack running off with the harp.

Listening Comprehension

Why does Jack go back up the beanstalk after he already had the golden hen?

practice

Define: *Practice* is doing something many times in order to get better at it.

Example: The soccer team has *practice* every day.

Ask: What is something that takes a lot of *practice* to be good at?

Listening Comprehension

What happens to the giant man at the end of the story?

The giant man chased after Jack and roared,

Fee-fum-fo-fi,
I will get you by and by!

Jack ran as fast as he could until he arrived at the beanstalk. He climbed down and he climbed down and he climbed down, as fast as he could. The giant swung himself down onto the beanstalk, too.

Jack had a lot more **practice** with climbing than the giant did, so he arrived with time to spare. He got hold of an ax and chopped the beanstalk in two. The giant fell out of the sky, straight through the earth. He was never heard from again.

Jack and his mother became very rich from showing the golden harp and selling the golden eggs. And they lived happily ever after.

Respond to the Story

Retell: Use the prompts on the back of the Retelling Cards to help children retell the story.

Think About It

1. What are some things that Jack did that show that he was brave?

2. The story says that Jack lived "happily ever after." What does that mean? What do you imagine Jack did next?

Activity: Have children draw a picture of Jack next to a picture of one of the giants. Invite them to try speaking in Jack's voice, and in a giant's voice. Help them to use comparing words to describe the differences between the two characters.

The Johnny Cake Boy

A Tale from Appalachia

Once an old woman made a johnnycake for her little boy's supper. She flattened it out on a board and put it over the fire to bake. Then she went out to **fetch** a bucket of water.

"Look after this johnnycake while I'm gone," the old woman said to her boy.

But almost as soon as she left the cabin, she heard her boy holler.

"Ma! Ma! That johnnycake is running away."

And sure enough, the old woman looked up and saw the johnnycake rolling off down the road with her boy running right after him. She dropped her bucket and took off after him, too.

The johnnycake rolled and rolled. He rolled past some men working at a mill.

"Where are you rolling off to, Johnny Cake?" the men hollered.

Johnny Cake rolled on past and sang out,

I'm rollin', rollin'
On my way
To see the world.
I cannot stay!

The men dropped their tools and took off after him.

Johnny Cake rolled and rolled. He rolled past a hog digging in the road.

The hog said, "Oomph! Oomph! Where are you rolling off to, Johnny Cake?"

WONDERFUL WORD

fetch

Define: *Fetch* means to go to get something and bring it back.
Example: The dog ran to *fetch* the ball.
Ask: What else could a dog *fetch*?

Listening Comprehension

How do you think the little boy felt when he saw Johnny Cake get up and run out? How would you feel?

Johnny Cake rolled on past and sang out,

I'm rollin', rollin'
On my way
To see the world.
I cannot stay!

The hog dropped the acorn it was chewing and took off after him.

Johnny Cake rolled and rolled. He came to a dog barking at a tree.

"Bow-wow!" said the dog. "Where are you rolling off to, Johnny Cake?"

Johnny Cake just rolled on past and sang out,

I'm rollin', rollin'
On my way
To see the world.
I cannot stay!

The dog stopped barking at the tree and took off after him.

Johnny Cake rolled and rolled. Soon he came to a goose that was **occupied** with eating grass.

"Honk, honk," said the goose. "Where are you rolling off to, Johnny Cake?"

Johnny Cake just rolled on past and sang out,

I'm rollin', rollin'
On my way
To see the world.
I cannot stay!

So the goose stopped eating the grass and took off after him.

Soon Johnny Cake came to a fox sitting on the bank of a river licking its lips.

The Johnny Cake Boy 49

"Where are you rolling off to, Johnny Cake?" the fox wanted to know.

Johnny Cake looked at the river and sang out,

I'm rollin', rollin'
Can't be slow
But through that river
I cannot go!

"Don't pay that river any mind at all," said the fox. "Hop on top of my head and I will swim you across."

So Johnny Cake did. But what do you know? Halfway across the river, that fox **dunked** his head in the water and Johnny Cake slid right off.

The fox grabbed Johnny Cake in its mouth and ate him all up!

Boo hoo! Johnny Cake was done going places and now so is this tale.

Listening Comprehension

How does Johnny Cake's rhyme change when he gets to the river? Why does it change?

WONDERFUL WORD

dunked

Define: *Dunked* means put quickly into water or another liquid.

Example: Leila *dunked* her bread into her milk.

Ask: How do ducks look when they *dunk* their heads in the water?

Respond to the Story

Retell: Use the prompts on the back of the Retelling Cards to help children retell the story.

Think About It

1. How did the fox trick Johnny Cake? How do you think the others felt when the fox ate Johnny Cake?

2. What was Johnny Cake like? What made him special?

Activity: Invite children to make johnnycake boys and girls out of clay or dough made with flour and water. Have them use buttons, clay, or other materials to give their johnnycakes a face like the one in the story. Have them use their johnnycakes to act out the story.

The Knee-High Man

An African American Tale

Once there lived a knee-high man. He was called that because he was no taller than a person's knees. The knee-high man didn't like being so short. He didn't like it in the least. In fact his greatest **goal** in life was to be as tall as everyone else.

One day the knee-high man decided to ask a large animal how to become big. So he went to visit the horse that lived down the road.

"Sister Horse," said the knee-high man. "I am sick of being so little. How can I get to be as big as you are?"

Sister Horse tapped her foot as she thought. Finally she said, "Eat a whole lot of apples. Then run around the meadow as many times as you can. After a while you'll be big and strong like me."

So the knee-high man did exactly as Sister Horse said. He ate apples until his belly got so big he couldn't see his shoes. Then he ran around the meadow so many times that soon he couldn't move.

But he didn't grow a single inch.

"Sister Horse doesn't know a thing about getting big," he decided. So he went to ask Brother Bull.

"Brother Bull," he said, "I'm sick and tired of being so little. How can I get to be as big as you are?"

Brother Bull stroked his chin and thought. Then he said, "Eat as much grass as you can. Then take a deep breath and let out a bellow. Do it a few times. That will make you big and strong like me."

WONDERFUL WORD

goal
Define: A *goal* is something important you plan to have, do, or be.
Example: My *goal* is to play one hour every day.
Ask: What are some of your *goals*?

Listening Comprehension

Why does the knee-high man think that Sister Horse can help him with his problem?

Listening Comprehension

Why is Brother Bull's advice silly?

WONDERFUL WORD

defend

Define: To *defend* is to keep safe from danger.
Example: The mother duck is careful to *defend* her eggs from other animals.
Ask: In the winter, how do you *defend* yourself against the cold?

So the knee-high man did exactly as Brother Bull said. He ate grass until he was so stuffed he couldn't even think about eating more. Then he roared and shouted as loud as he could. But all he ended up with was a stomachache and a sore throat. And he didn't grow a single inch.

"Sister Horse and Brother Bull are the two biggest creatures around," said the knee-high man. "If they don't know how to get big, then no one does."

Just then he heard an owl hooting. The knee-high man remembered that owls know just about everything.

"Brother Owl," he said, "You are wise. How can I get to be big like Sister Horse and Brother Bull?"

"What do you want to be big for?" Brother Owl asked. "What's the problem with being little?"

"I want to be big so that when someone wants to hurt me, I can **defend** myself," said the knee-high man.

Brother Owl looked around. "Who's been hurting you, knee-high man?" he asked.

"Well, nobody has, Brother Owl," answered the knee-high man.

"Then why do you have to defend yourself?" asked Brother Owl.

The knee-high man scratched his chin. He thought and he thought a little more.

"But Brother Owl," he said, "I need to be big so I can see far away."

"Climb up this tree and you will be able to see anything you need to see, just like I can," said Brother Owl.

The knee-high man did just that. And from then on, he was **content** with his size.

Listening Comprehension

Is Brother Owl big like Sister Horse and Brother Bull? Why does the knee-high man ask him for help?

Respond to the Story

Retell: Use the prompts on the back of the Retelling Cards to help children retell the story.

Think About It

1. What lesson did the knee-high man learn from Brother Owl?

2. What are some things that the knee-high man might enjoy about being small?

Activity: Have children draw self-portraits, highlighting their favorite features (hair, face, etc.). Invite them to explain why they are content with the way they are.

WONDERFUL WORD

content

Define: *Content* means happy with what you are and have.
Example: I was hungry all morning. Then I had a sandwich and was finally *content*.
Ask: When do you feel *content*?

The Lion and the Mouse

A Fable by Aesop

One day a great lion was sleeping when a little mouse scurried by. The mouse was so busy searching for food that she walked onto the lion's paw by mistake. This woke up the lion, and before the little mouse knew what had happened, the lion was holding her tight.

"What a tasty snack you will make, little mouse," said the lion. He lifted the mouse up to his mouth and opened his huge jaws.

"Oh, pardon me, Great King Lion," said the mouse. "Please do not eat me. I will never do anything to **disturb** you again. And if you help me, one of these days, I may be able to help you, too."

"YOU!" said the lion. "How will YOU ever be able to help ME? You are far too little and weak."

"Size has nothing to do with it," said the mouse. "Let me go and you will see. A little friend may be a great friend."

The lion was so amused at the idea of a tiny mouse being able to help him that he gently set her down upon the ground.

Not long after, the lion was caught in a trap. The hunter who caught him wanted to bring him to the king. He had tied the lion to a tree while he went to get help. The lion roared with all of his might.

Just then the little mouse happened to pass by. "What has happened to you, my big friend?" asked the mouse.

The lion stopped roaring at once. He remembered the little mouse.

"A hunter caught me in a trap and is waiting to take me to the king," said the lion. "My days of **wandering** free are past."

"I can help you!" said the mouse. At once she started to chew on the rope. She chewed and chewed until at last the rope broke and the lion was free.

The lion thanked the mouse and prepared to run away.

"You were right, little mouse," he said. "A little friend may be a great friend indeed!"

Listening Comprehension

How do you think the lion feels when he gets caught?

WONDERFUL WORD

wandering
Define: *Wandering* is moving or walking wherever one wishes.
Example: Maggie likes *wandering* around the library, looking for interesting books.
Ask: Which is a good place for *wandering*, the park or the kitchen?

Respond to the Story

Retell: Use the prompts on the back of the Retelling Cards to help children retell the story.

Think About It

1. How did the mouse show that she was a good friend to the lion?

2. If the lion was so big and strong, why couldn't he get out of the trap himself? Explain why the mouse's size may have actually helped her free the lion.

Activity: Invite children to tell about a time when someone helped them. Then have them make thank-you cards for the people to thank them for being good friends.

Little Juan and the Cooking Pot

A Tale from Puerto Rico

Listening Comprehension

How does Little Juan feel about bringing the cooking pot from Abuela's? What does that tell you about him?

WONDERFUL WORD

sensible

Define: *Sensible* means to have good judgment or sense.

Example: It is *sensible* to wear a raincoat in the rain.

Ask: What is *sensible* to wear when it is cold out?

Once there was a boy named Little Juan who lived with his mama. Like many boys, Little Juan liked to play more than he liked to work. And when he wasn't playing, he liked to lay in the hammock and daydream.

"Little Juan," said Mama one day. "I am making a big stew for dinner but all I have is this little pot. Can you run to Abuela Carmen's and borrow her big cooking pot?"

"Ay, Mama," said Little Juan. "Do I have to?"

"Little Juan," said Mama. "Do you want your dinner?"

And of course Little Juan did. So he ran up the hill and down the hill all the way to Abuela Carmen's.

"You may borrow my pot, Little Juan," said Abuela. "But remember to take good care of it. You are not always a **sensible** boy."

"Don't worry, Abuela," said Little Juan. "You can trust me."

Abuela Carmen handed Little Juan her pot. Now it was a very old-fashioned pot. It had three legs so that it could stand in the fireplace. And it was so large and heavy that Little Juan could barely lift it.

Little Juan hadn't walked very far at all when he had to set the pot down. He sat next to it on the road. He looked at the pot. He counted.

"One leg, two legs, three legs," he said. He started to think. "Pot," he said. "Why is it that you have three legs and I only have two legs and yet I am the one who is carrying you?"

The pot did not answer.

Little Juan stood up. "Pot," he said. "I can see that you do not have a mouth, so I do not **expect** you to talk. But you do have three legs, so I am sure you can walk."

The pot did not answer and it did not move. Little Juan climbed inside the pot.

"Pot," he said. "With so many legs, I am sure you can walk much better than I can. You may bring me home now."

He lay back and put his feet up on the pot's rim. He fell asleep. When he woke up a little while later, he noticed that the pot had not moved an inch.

"Pot," he said. "It is clear that you do not want to carry me home. But surely you do not think I should carry you home!"

He climbed out of the pot. He gave the pot a push. "Go ahead, walk!" he commanded.

But the pot did not answer and it did not move.

Little Juan looked at the pot.

"I know!" he said at last. "We will have a race. Even though you have three legs and I only have two, I will run my fastest and may still beat you. The winner will have a taste of cane syrup."

WONDERFUL WORD

expect
Define: *Expect* means to think something will happen.
Example: In the winter, I *expect* it to be cold.
Ask: What do you *expect* you will do after you get up tomorrow?

Listening Comprehension

Why does Little Juan think that the pot can walk?

prepared
Define: *Prepared* means to get ready.
Example: Sam *prepared* for bed by brushing his teeth.
Ask: How do you *prepare* for bed?

Listening Comprehension

Why does Little Juan expect to see the pot at home? Where is the pot?

The pot did not answer and it did not move.

But Little Juan squatted down beside the pot and **prepared** to race. "One, two, three, go!" he shouted.

Then he ran off as fast as he could. He ran up the hill and down the hill. He never once looked back for fear of seeing the pot beating him.

At last he got home.

"Mama!" he cried, out of breath. "Did it come yet? Did it beat me?"

"Did what beat you, Little Juan?" asked Mama. "And where is the cooking pot?"

Little Juan told Mama about the pot, its legs, and the race.

"Oh my, Little Juan," Mama said. "You are such a silly boy! Whatever shall become of you?"

Little Juan hung his head. Then he patted his belly. "But, Mama," he said. "What about the stew?"

"Come let us go down the hill and get the pot together," said Mama. "We will have a very late dinner tonight."

"I hope the pot does not want to eat too much," said Little Juan.

Mama took Little Juan by the hand and smiled. And then they set off to get the pot.

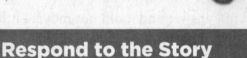

Respond to the Story

Retell: Use the prompts on the back of the Retelling Cards to help children retell the story.

Think About It

1. What makes this story silly? What silly things does Little Juan do?

2. What would you have done if you had been Little Juan?

Activity: Little Juan's mama was making his favorite stew in the big cooking pot. Find a large box or container. Have children draw a picture of a kind of food they like and place it in the container. Reread the story and invite children to take turns pretending to be Little Juan carrying the "pot."

The Little Red Hen

A Tale from England

WONDERFUL WORD

cozy
Define: *Cozy* means comfortable.
Example: The reading corner of our classroom is very *cozy*.
Ask: What places do you find *cozy*?

Listening Comprehension

What is the little red hen like? How is she different from her friends?

Once upon a time a dog, a cat, a mouse, and a little red hen all lived together in a **cozy** little house. One day, the little red hen found some grains of wheat in the yard.

"Who will plant this wheat?" asked the little red hen.

"Not I," said the dog.

"Not I," said the cat.

"Not I," said the mouse.

"Then I will do it myself," said the little red hen. And she did.

The wheat grew taller and taller. It turned from green to gold. At last it was time to cut the wheat. "The wheat is ripe," said the little red hen. "Who will help me cut it?"

"Not I," said the dog.

"Not I," said the cat.

"Not I," said the mouse.

"Then I will do it myself," said the little red hen. And she did.

After the wheat was cut, it was ready to be ground into flour.

"Who will take this wheat to the mill?" asked the little red hen.

"Not I," said the dog.

"Not I," said the cat.

"Not I," said the mouse.

Listening
Comprehension

Do you think the little
red hen will let her
friends share the bread?
Why or why not?

WONDERFUL WORD

intend

Define: If you *intend* to do
something, it means you
are planning to do it.
Example: I *intend* to have
a glass of milk as soon as I
get home.
Ask: What do you *intend*
to do first when you
get home?

"Then I will do it myself," said the little red hen. And she did.

The little red hen carried the flour back to her house. "Who will help me make this flour into bread?" asked the little red hen.

"Not I," said the dog.

"Not I," said the cat.

"Not I," said the mouse.

"Then I will do it myself," said the little red hen. And she did.

Soon the bread was ready. "Who will help me eat this superb bread?" asked the little red hen as she took it out of the oven.

"I will!" said the dog.

"I will!" said the cat.

"I will!" said the mouse.

"Oh, no you will not!" said the little red hen. "You did not help me plant the wheat. You did not help me cut the wheat. You did not help me take the wheat to the mill. You did not help me bake the bread. And now you are not going to help me eat. I **intend** to eat it all by myself."

And she did.

Respond to the Story

Retell: Use the prompts on the back of the Retelling Cards to help children retell the story.

Think About It

1. Do you think the little red hen was right not to share the bread? Why or why not?

2. What lesson do you think the other animals learned? Do you think they will be more willing to help out next time?

Activity: Invite children to draw one of the animals from the story. Show them how to add a speech balloon. Help them write the words "Not I."

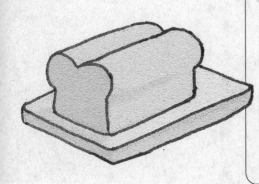

Little Red Riding Hood

A Tale from Germany

Once upon a time, there was a good little girl who always wore a red cloak with a hood, so everyone called her Little Red Riding Hood.

One day, her mother said to her, "Grandmother is not feeling well. **Deliver** this basket of bread and cheese to her to make her feel better. Do not stray or talk to strangers on the way."

"I won't, Mother," said Little Red Riding Hood.

Grandmother lived in the woods, not far from the village. Little Red Riding Hood was walking through the woods when she met a wolf.

"Good morning," said the wolf. "Where are you going?"

"I am taking this basket to Grandmother."

"Where does she live?" asked the wolf.

"Her house is on this path, under three big oak trees," said Little Red Riding Hood.

The wolf thought, "This girl would make a mighty fine snack. But if I am clever, I can feast on the grandmother, too."

WONDERFUL WORD

deliver
Define: *Deliver* means take something to someone.
Example: The pizza shop will *deliver* the pizza to our house.
Ask: What gets *delivered* to your home?

Listening Comprehension

Why does the wolf want to know where Grandmother lives?

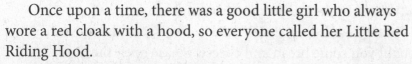

They walked along together for a while. Then the wolf said, "Look at all the pretty wildflowers. Perhaps Grandmother would like some."

Little Red Riding Hood looked at the bright flowers. "Yes, Grandmother likes flowers very much," she thought. So she picked one, and then another, wandering farther and farther from the path.

While Little Red Riding Hood was picking flowers, the wolf ran to Grandmother's cottage and knocked on the door.

"Who is there?" called Grandmother.

"Little Red Riding Hood," said the wolf, in a dainty voice. "I've brought you some bread and cheese. Please open the door!"

"I am too weak to get up," called Grandmother. "Lift the latch."

The wolf lifted the latch and the door flew open. He **entered** the cottage and ate up Grandmother. Then he put on her nightgown and nightcap, got into bed, and pulled up the covers.

Little Red Riding Hood picked flowers until she could carry no more. Then she went to Grandmother's cottage. When she got there, she was surprised to see that the door stood open.

"Good morning, Grandmother," she called. There was no answer. She went to the bed. There lay Grandmother, but she looked very strange.

"Grandmother, what big ears you have," said Little Red Riding Hood.

"The better to hear you with, my dear."

"Grandmother, what big eyes you have."

"The better to see you with, my dear."

"Grandmother, what big teeth you have."

"The better to EAT you with," said the wolf.

At that, he jumped out of bed and swallowed poor Little Red Riding Hood. Then he went back to bed and was soon snoring loudly.

A hunter went past the house and thought, "How loudly Old Grandmother is snoring. I must see if there is anything the matter with her." He went in and saw the wolf lying on Grandmother's bed.

"But where is Old Grandmother?" he wondered. Suddenly, he **realized** that the wolf had swallowed her whole! "Maybe I can save her," he thought.

Now the wolf was sleeping very deeply, so the hunter slowly and carefully opened his jaws very wide to see if there was anyone inside.

Out jumped Grandmother, followed by Little Red Riding Hood.

The hunter took the wolf away, and made sure that he would never bother anyone again. Grandmother ate the bread and cheese, and soon felt strong.

Little Red Riding Hood went back home without straying or talking to strangers, just as her mother had told her.

Respond to the Story

Retell: Use the prompts on the back of the Retelling Cards to help children retell the story.

Think About It

1. Why did the wolf dress up as Grandmother? Do you think his plan was a good one? Why or why not?

2. What do you think Little Red Riding Hood learned by the end of the story? What will she do differently next time?

Activity: Little Red Riding Hood notices the wolf's big teeth. Have children cut out pictures of animals from magazines. Divide a piece of chart paper into three columns. Label the columns *Big Teeth, Small Teeth, No Teeth*. Paste each animal picture on the appropriate column. Repeat with *Big Ears, Small Ears, No Ears*.

Mouse Deer Crosses the River

A Tale from Malaysia

Mouse Deer may have been little, but he walked around the jungle just like he owned it. When he wasn't munching on leaves, he was running and jumping and generally causing trouble. And when he got bored with that, he went to the river to gaze at his own reflection. As he looked at himself, he sang,

My head is like a mouse.
My legs are like a deer.
I'm the best-looking animal
Far or near.

While he was indeed a fine-looking animal, it was Mouse Deer's brain that was his greatest strength.

One day Mouse Deer saw a **splendid** piece of fruit hanging from a tree on the other side of the river.

"Now that looks tasty," he said. "I wish fruit like that grew on *my* side of the river."

"What is that, little Mouse Deer?" came a voice. It was Crocodile.

Now there were many animals that wanted to eat Mouse Deer, but crocodiles were the biggest and the meanest. Mouse Deer took a large step backward.

"That was close, little Mouse Deer," said Crocodile, with her big teeth showing. "Someday you will forget yourself and come into the river. And then you will be my dinner."

Mouse Deer turned and ran. When he was at a safe distance, he called out,

I'm as smart as smart can be.
No crocodile will ever eat me!

That night Mouse Deer kept thinking about the fruit on the other side of the river. And the more he thought about it, the more he wanted it. There had to be a way to get to it without Crocodile eating him.

The next morning Mouse Deer went back to the river. "Good day, Crocodile," he called. "I, Mouse Deer, am crossing the river. You can eat me if you want. But if you do, then my one hundred cousins will come and eat you up."

Crocodile's head popped out of the water. "Then *my* one hundred cousins will eat *your* one hundred cousins," she said. "You give them that warning!"

"You don't have a hundred cousins!" said Mouse Deer. "Everyone knows there are no other crocodiles in this river."

Crocodile was so astonished she spat. "No crocodiles?" she cried. "You are mistaken, my friend. I have many, many cousins who would swim to my **aid** at a moment's notice!"

"Prove it," said Mouse Deer. "If you have even ten cousins, I will jump in the river now so that you can eat me."

"With pleasure," said Crocodile. She let out a shout and soon many crocodiles swam up to greet her.

Mouse Deer started to count, "One crocodile, two crocodiles, three crocodiles, . . ." Then he shook his head. "This is getting confusing," he said. "Why don't all of you crocodiles line up? That way I can be sure to count each one of you. Start here and make a row to the other side of the river."

"Good thinking!" said Crocodile, licking her lips and thinking about what a tasty meal Mouse Deer would make.

The crocodiles lined up in a neat row that reached from one side of the river to the other.

WONDERFUL WORD

aid
Define: *Aid* means help.
Example: The nurse came to my *aid* when I fell.
Ask: How would you *aid* a kitten stuck in a tree?

Listening Comprehension

Why does Crocodile call all her cousins? Do you think Mouse Deer wanted her to? Why?

WONDERFUL WORD

single

Define: *Single* means one; not part of a pair or group.
Example: There was not a *single* marker left for Juan to use.
Ask: Why is having only a *single* mitten a problem?

Listening Comprehension

Why does Mouse Deer ask the crocodiles to line up? What do the crocodiles think is the reason?

"Excellent!" said Mouse Deer. "When I tap each of you on the back, you will have been counted. Now stay very still."

Mouse Deer hopped onto the first crocodile. "One crocodile!" he called. Then he hopped on the next. "Two crocodiles!" he called. He hopped onto the third crocodile. "Three crocodiles!" he called.

"Ha, ha, little Mouse Deer," said Crocodile. "You will see there are more of us than you thought."

"Hold still," Mouse Deer told the crocodiles. "I don't want to miss a **single** one of you."

Mouse Deer hopped from crocodile to crocodile until he reached the very last one. "Ten Crocodiles!" he called. "Why, Crocodile, you were right!"

"Of course I was right," called Crocodile. "Foolish Mouse Deer, prepare to be eaten."

But just then Mouse Deer hopped off the last crocodile and onto the land. He had crossed the river!

He ran up the hill. Then he called out, "There certainly are a lot of crocodiles in the river and each of you is more foolish than the last. I made it to the other side of the river and I think I will stay for a while. Thank you so much for helping me!"

Then Mouse Deer skipped off to find that splendid piece of fruit.

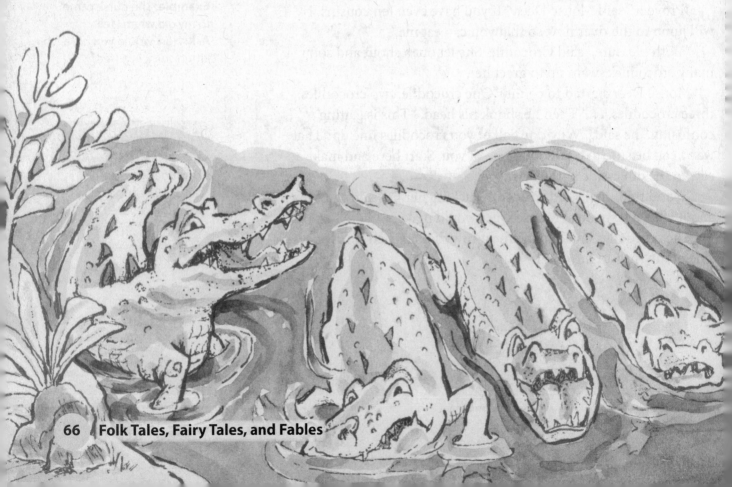

Respond to the Story

Retell: Use the prompts on the back of the Retelling Cards to help children retell the story.

Think About It

1. What did Mouse Deer mean when he said that each of the crocodiles was more foolish than the last?

2. What kind of character is Mouse Deer? How would you describe him?

Activity: Have children count their way across the river like Mouse Deer did. Use yarn or another marker to designate two banks of a river. Give children sets of counters. Have them lay the counters from one end of the river to the other. Then they can pretend to be Mouse Deer counting off each "crocodile" as they cross the river. Vary the distance between the shores and have children predict how many counters it will take to cross.

Now Things Are Worse!

A Yiddish Tale

Listening Comprehension

What is Sam and Sara's problem? How could they solve it?

WONDERFUL WORD

commotion

Define: *Commotion* means a lot of noisy and excited activity.

Example: There was a big *commotion* on the soccer field after Jack scored the winning goal.

Ask: What does a *commotion* sound like?

Many years ago a poor couple named Sam and Sara lived together in a tiny one-room cottage. Sam and Sara were bakers. Each morning they baked dozens of loaves of bread in a wood-burning oven in the middle of the cottage, to sell at the market.

But Sam and Sara had a problem. They did not live alone. They lived with their six children, Sam's parents, a dog, and a cat.

The cottage was always noisy. The children argued. The grownups shouted. The dog barked and the cat meowed.

The cottage was always messy. The children left clothes on the floor. The grownups left pots on the stove. The dog and cat made muddy tracks.

The cottage was always hectic. The children ran, played, and cried. The grownups cooked, ate, and worked. The dog got into the garbage and the cat got into the mending.

One morning Sara had had enough of the **commotion**. "I can't take it anymore!" she said to Sam. "This cottage is too noisy, too messy, and too hectic. We can hardly manage to bake our bread! Go ask the wise man. He will tell us what to do."

Sam went to see the wise man. "Wise man," said Sam. "My wife and I are desperate for help. We live in a tiny cottage with our six children, my parents, a dog, and a cat. There is so much commotion that we can hardly get our work done. We are miserable!"

The wise man nodded his head and tugged his beard. Then he asked, "Do you have any animals?"

"Well, yes," said Sam proudly. "We have two chickens, a goat, and a cow."

"Do as I say," said the wise man. "Bring the chickens inside the cottage to live with you."

Sam thought this was very strange advice, but he did as the wise man said.

The chickens clucked all through the day and night. They flapped their wings and jumped on the table. Their feathers fell on the floor and stuck to the walls.

After a few days, Sam and Sara could not stand it any longer.

Sam returned to the wise man. "Wise man," said Sam, "I did **exactly** as you told me and brought the chickens into our home. But now things are worse! We can hardly sleep with all of the flapping and clucking. There are feathers in the bread! We are miserable!"

WONDERFUL WORD

exactly
Define: *Exactly* means just the same.
Example: My sister always copies me. She does *exactly* what I do.
Ask: How are all cats *exactly* alike?

Listening Comprehension

What happens when Sam brings the chickens into the house?

Now Things Are Worse! **69**

Listening Comprehension

Why do you think the wise man is telling them to bring animals into the house? How could that help?

The wise man raised his hand and said, "Do as I say. Bring the goat inside to live with you."

"Has he lost his mind?" thought Sam. "Who wants to live with a goat?" Even so, Sam did as the wise man said.

The goat bleated loudly all through the day and night. It ran wild around the cottage, butting into the furniture and the children. It chewed up the family's clothes. The chickens continued to cluck and flap and spread feathers everywhere.

After a few days, Sam and Sara could not stand it any longer.

Sam returned to the wise man. "Wise man," said Sam. "I did exactly as you told me and brought the goat into our home. But now things are worse! The crazy goat eats everything we have! It bleats loudly and runs wild! And still the chickens make a racket and a mess. We are miserable!"

The wise man looked Sam in the eye and said, "Do as I say. Bring the cow inside to live with you."

"Not the cow!" thought Sam. "We cannot live with a cow!" Even so, Sam did as the wise man said.

"Not the cow!" cried Sara when Sam brought the cow into the cottage.

The cow mooed all through the day and night. It crashed into the chairs and even broke some. The goat continued to bleat and chew and run wild. The chickens continued to cluck and flap and spread feathers everywhere. The cottage was messier, noisier, and more hectic than ever!

Sam and Sara could not stand it any longer.

Sam called for the wise man. "Wise man," said Sam, "I did exactly as you told me and brought the cow into our home. But now things are even worse! Our home has become a barnyard! My family cannot live with animals anymore!"

"You're absolutely right!" said the wise man. "Take all of the animals out of your home."

Sam did as the wise man said.

With all of the animals out, the cottage felt very quiet, clean, and **peaceful**. Sam and Sara were able to bake their bread. The children played nicely together. The grandparents took a nap. "How can we ever thank you enough?" Sara said to the wise man. "You have made life sweet for us."

Respond to the Story

Retell: Use the prompts on the back of the Retelling Cards to help children retell the story.

Think About It

1. Why did things get worse and worse in the cottage?

2. How did the wise man help Sam and Sara? What made them feel better about life in their cottage?

Activity: Invite children to draw pictures of Sam and Sara's cottage when it is most hectic. Then have them draw pictures showing their cottage when it is peaceful. Have them dictate sentences to you about their drawings.

Rabbit and Coyote's Big Race
A Pueblo Tale

Listening Comprehension

Who do you think will win the race, the rabbit or the coyote? Why?

WONDERFUL WORD

relatives

Define: *Relatives* are members of a family.
Example: Many of Sam's *relatives* came to his party, including his brothers and cousins.
Ask: Which of your *relatives* live with you?

One day, in the hot desert, a cottontail rabbit was sitting under a large cactus plant when a coyote came running by.

When the coyote spotted the rabbit, he stopped. "Hello, little friend," he said. "What are you doing?"

"I'm just sitting here thinking about why coyotes have long tails," said the rabbit. "Doesn't your long tail slow you down when you run?"

"Not at all," replied the coyote. "I can run faster than any animal in the desert."

"Well then, perhaps we should have a race next week," said the rabbit.

"Good idea!" the coyote said. "We'll race to the four corners of the land. And the winner gets to eat the loser!" he added.

The rabbit agreed. That night, he sent for his **relatives** from the four corners of the land. All the rabbits made a plan to work together to beat the coyote in the race.

On the day of the race, the coyote met the rabbit by the cactus plant again. "Are you ready, little friend?" asked the coyote. "Or should I just eat you now and save time?"

"Let's race!" said the rabbit. "You can run across the land, and I will run underground, because I can run faster that way. We'll see who is the fastest."

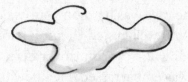

"Ready . . . set . . . go!" called the two runners. Then they ran off. The coyote ran across the sweltering desert, and the rabbit hopped a few times before disappearing into his burrow.

The coyote ran east for many days, and did not see the rabbit anywhere. Then, just as he arrived at the eastern corner of the land, a rabbit jumped up from a hole in the ground.

"Looks like I got here first!" said the rabbit. Then the rabbit dived back down into the hole. What the coyote didn't know was that this was the first rabbit's sister!

The coyote turned and started to run north. He ran north for many days. When he arrived at the northern corner of the land, a rabbit poked his head out of the ground.

"I beat you again!" said the rabbit. What the coyote didn't know was this was the first rabbit's brother!

Now the coyote was determined to win. He ran west as fast as he could. He ran for many days. But when he arrived at the western corner of the land, a rabbit jumped out of the ground again.

"Slowpoke!" teased the rabbit. What the coyote didn't know was that this was the first rabbit's cousin!

Turning south, the coyote ran and ran. Of course, when he reached the southern corner of the land, a rabbit popped up in front of him. What he didn't know was that this was the first rabbit's uncle!

Now the coyote turned to go back home. He was worn out! It took him days to limp back to the starting point of the race. When he finally arrived, the first rabbit was there to **greet** him.

Rabbit and Coyote's Big Race   **73**

WONDERFUL WORD

relaxed

Define: Someone who is *relaxed* is calm and well-rested.

Example: I always feel *relaxed* during summer vacation.

Ask: When do you feel *relaxed*?

Listening Comprehension

Explain why the coyote is embarrassed at the end.

"I see that the race was hard on you!" said the rabbit, who looked **relaxed** and well-rested. "I guess a long tail really does slow an animal down! Now come over here, and I will eat you."

The coyote was embarrassed. He knew the rabbit would not really eat him, but he ran away as fast as he could. As he ran, he tucked his long tail between his legs.

Then the rabbit sent word to his relatives that together they had beaten the coyote!

Respond to the Story

Retell: Use the prompts on the back of the Retelling Cards to help children retell the story.

Think About It

1. Where was the first rabbit during the race?

2. Do you think what the rabbits did was fair? Why?

Activity: Have each child use clay or dough to make a rabbit. Using small paper cups as "rabbit holes," have groups of children enact the story with one child and rabbit at each hole. Children can take turns being the coyote.

The Rooster Who Went to Tío's Wedding

A Tale from Cuba

Once upon a time, there was a rooster whose Tío, or uncle, was getting married. Rooster put on his best suit for the wedding. Then he set off, feeling very proud and fine.

While he was walking, Rooster noticed two plump corn kernels lying in the mud. Now, he was terribly hungry and wanted very much to eat those two little pieces of corn. But if he ate them, his beak would get muddy, and then he would not look his best for the wedding. Rooster tried hard to **resist**, but could not, and he gobbled up the two kernels in an instant.

"What shall I do now?" crowed Rooster, for his beak was indeed covered with mud. He could not go to Tío's wedding looking such a mess!

He decided to ask Grass for help. "Sweet Grass, wipe the mud from my beak so that I can go to Tío's wedding," he said.

Grass replied, "No, I won't."

Rooster looked around and spotted Cow. "Helpful Cow," said Rooster,

Eat the grass
that won't wipe my beak
so that I can go to Tío's wedding.

WONDERFUL WORD

resist

Define: To *resist* is to stop yourself from doing something that you want to do.
Example: Theo wanted a second slice of pizza, but he decided to *resist* because he was full.
Ask: What foods do you find hard to *resist*?

Listening Comprehension

What is the cause of Rooster's problem?

WONDERFUL WORD

attend

Define: To *attend* is to go to an event.
Example: Felicia hopes that all of her friends will *attend* her party.
Ask: When did you last *attend* a family event? Tell about it.

Listening Comprehension

Everyone who Rooster asks for help replies the same way. What do they all say to him?

Cow replied, "No, I won't."
Rooster kept walking until he saw Dog. "Brave Dog," said Rooster,

> **Bite the cow**
> **that won't eat the grass**
> **that won't wipe my beak**
> **so that I can go to Tío's wedding.**

Dog replied, "No, I won't."
It was getting late, but Rooster was still determined to **attend** Tío's wedding. He spotted a stick near the road. "Strong Stick," said Rooster,

> **Hit the dog**
> **that won't bite the cow**
> **that won't eat the grass**
> **that won't wipe my beak**
> **so that I can go to Tío's wedding.**

Stick replied, "No, I won't."
Rooster was upset, but he would not give up. He saw a campfire on a nearby hill. "Hot Fire," said Rooster,

> **Burn the stick**
> **that won't hit the dog**
> **that won't bite the cow**
> **that won't eat the grass**
> **that won't wipe my beak**
> **so that I can go to Tío's wedding.**

Fire replied, "No, I won't."

"What will I do?" worried Rooster. Just then he came across a small stream. "Cool Water," said Rooster,

> **Put out the fire**
> **that won't burn the stick**
> **that won't hit the dog**
> **that won't bite the cow**
> **that won't eat the grass**
> **that won't wipe my beak**
> **so that I can go to Tío's wedding.**

Water replied, "No, I won't."

Rooster was feeling desperate. He did not know who else to ask for help. So he lifted his head and crowed. That's when he noticed his good friend Sol, the sun, high up in the sky. Every morning Rooster sang to him, to wake him up.

"Please, warm Sol," said Rooster,

> **Dry the water**
> **that won't put out the fire**
> **that won't burn the stick**
> **that won't hit the dog**
> **that won't bite the cow**
> **that won't eat the grass**
> **that won't wipe my beak**
> **so that I can go to Tío's wedding.**

Listening Comprehension

Why do you think no one wants to help Rooster?

WONDERFUL WORD

relieved

Define: A person feels *relieved* when his or her problems have been solved, or when everything turns out fine.

Example: Jimmy dropped a glass, but felt *relieved* because it didn't break.

Ask: Which would make you feel *relieved*, finding your favorite toy that had been lost, or spilling a drink on your shirt?

"*Por supuesto*, old friend," said Sol. "Of course I'll help you."

Now, Water heard Sol's reply and said, "Please don't dry me! I'll put out the fire."

Fire heard it too and said, "I'll burn the stick!"

Then Stick said, "I will hit the dog!"

Then Dog said, "I will bite the cow!"

Cow said, "I will eat the grass!"

Finally Grass shouted, "Please don't eat me! I will wipe the mud from Rooster's beak."

And he did.

Rooster was so **relieved**! He was proud of his shiny, clean beak, and was ready to go to Tío's wedding. But before he left, he made sure to thank Sol with a happy "Cock-a-doodle-doo!"

Respond to the Story

Retell: Use the prompts on the back of the Retelling Cards to help children retell the story.

Think About It

1. Describe Rooster's character. What kinds of things are important to him?

2. Why did Sol want to help Rooster? What made all of the others decide to help, too?

Activity: Enact the story as a group. Have each child play a character. Pin labels, with a picture and word (for example, "fire" or "dog") to children's shirts. Arrange the children in the correct sequential order. Have all children except the one whose character Rooster is addressing join in on the repetitive phrases.

The Three Bears

A Tale from England

A papa bear, a mama bear, and a baby bear lived together in a very **pleasant** cottage in the middle of a great big forest. Papa Bear was huge. Mama Bear was medium-size. Baby Bear was quite tiny.

One morning, the bears made porridge. But it was too hot to eat. So they went out for a walk while it cooled.

Just then a girl named Goldilocks came to their house. No one was home so she decided to go right in. "How hungry I am!" she said. "And how delicious that porridge smells!"

Goldilocks sat down at the table. She tasted some porridge from Papa Bear's bowl. But it was too hot. She tasted some porridge from Mama Bear's bowl. But it was too cold.

She tasted some porridge from Baby Bear's bowl. And it was just right. So she ate it all up.

Next, she went to the living room. She sat in Papa Bear's chair. But it was too hard. She sat in Mama Bear's chair. But it was too soft.

Then she sat in Baby Bear's chair. And it was just right.

WONDERFUL WORD

pleasant
Define: *Pleasant* means likeable or enjoyable.
Example: The park is a *pleasant* place for a picnic.
Ask: What is a *pleasant* place where you like to go?

Listening Comprehension

Why does Goldilocks go into the bears' house? What do you think she'll do next?

WONDERFUL WORD

exhausted
Define: *Exhausted* means very tired.
Example: After a long day at the beach, Shari was *exhausted*.
Ask: What activities make you feel *exhausted*?

"How comfortable I am!" said Goldilocks, bouncing up and down.

But she bounced around so much that the chair broke. Goldilocks fell right onto the floor.

Then she went to the bedroom. She got into Papa Bear's bed. But it was too high. She got into Mama Bear's bed. But it was too low. She got into Baby Bear's bed. And it was just right.

"How **exhausted** I am!" said Goldilocks. And she fell fast asleep.

Just then the three bears came home.

"Someone has been eating my porridge," shouted Papa Bear in his loud voice.

"Someone has been eating my porridge," said Mama Bear in her medium voice.

"Someone has been eating my porridge," squeaked Baby Bear in his soft voice. "And they have eaten it all up!"

They went into the living room.

"Someone has been sitting in my chair," shouted Papa Bear in his loud voice.

"Someone has been sitting in my chair," said Mama Bear in her medium voice.

"Someone has been sitting in my chair," squeaked Baby Bear in his soft voice. "And they have broken it all to bits."

Next, they went into the bedroom.

"Someone has been sleeping in my bed," shouted Papa Bear in his loud voice.

"Someone has been sleeping in my bed," said Mama Bear in her medium voice.

"Someone has been sleeping in my bed," squeaked Baby Bear in his soft voice. "And there she is now!"

Goldilocks woke up and was so **startled** by the three bears that she tumbled right out of bed. She ran out the door and all the way home. She never went back to the forest again!

Listening Comprehension

What clues tell the bears that someone has been in their house?

WONDERFUL WORD

startled

Define: *Startled* means very surprised.

Example: The birds left their nest when the loud thunder *startled* them.

Ask: Which might *startle* you, reading a book or being waked by a loud alarm clock?

Respond to the Story

Retell: Use the prompts on the back of the Retelling Cards to help children retell the story.

Think About It

1. Do you think that Goldilocks knew the house belonged to a family of bears? Would she have gone in if she knew?

2. Why do you think Goldilocks liked Baby Bear's things the best? What did they have in common?

Activity: Invite children to imagine how Goldilocks felt when she woke up and saw the three bears next to her. Have them dictate what they imagine Goldilocks might have said at that moment. Then have them draw portraits of Goldilocks that show how she was feeling.

The Three Billy Goats Gruff

A Tale from Norway

WONDERFUL WORD

pleaded

Define: *Pleaded* means begged or asked.
Example: Maria *pleaded* with her mom to let her play a little longer.
Ask: What is something that you have *pleaded* for?

Listening Comprehension

Why does the troll let the first two Billy Goats go? What do you think will happen when Big Billy walks across the bridge?

Once there were three Billy Goats whose last name was Gruff. The three brothers lived near a river. Across the river was a hillside where the grass was sweet. But the goats had to cross a bridge to get there, and a mean troll lived under it.

One day the brothers decided to cross the bridge. The youngest, smallest Billy Goat Gruff went first.

Trip-trap, trip-trap, went his feet as he crossed the bridge.

"WHO IS GOING OVER MY BRIDGE?" roared the troll.

"It is only I, Little Billy Goat Gruff," said Little Billy in a tiny voice.

"I'm going to gobble you up!" said the troll.

"Please don't do that!" **pleaded** Little Billy. "I'm too little. But here comes my brother, and he is much bigger than I am."

"Bigger, you say? Run along, then. I'll wait for a bigger meal," said the troll. So Little Billy ran across the bridge.

The second Billy Goat Gruff started to cross the bridge. Trip-trap, trip-trap, went his feet.

"WHO IS GOING OVER MY BRIDGE?" roared the troll.

"It is only I, Middle Billy Goat Gruff," said Middle Billy. His voice was louder than his little brother's.

"I'm going to gobble you up!" said the troll.

"Please don't do that!" pleaded Middle Billy. "My brother is right behind me, and he is much bigger than I am."

Now the troll was very hungry and was becoming impatient. But he said, "Very well, I'll wait for a bigger meal." And he let Middle Billy cross the bridge and join his little brother.

Then the oldest and biggest Billy Goat Gruff went across the bridge. TRIP-TRAP, TRIP-TRAP, went his feet. The bridge creaked as he walked across because this Billy Goat was so big and heavy.

"WHO IS GOING OVER MY BRIDGE?" roared the troll.

"IT IS I, BIG BILLY GOAT GRUFF!" said Big Billy in a booming voice.

"I'm going to gobble you up!" said the troll.

Big Billy Goat said bravely, "That's what you think!"

The troll climbed on the bridge, but Big Billy Goat Gruff was ready for him. He lowered his horns and butted the mean troll into the air! Then down, down, down the troll fell into the river below, and he was gone.

"Well, that takes care of the troll," said Big Billy, as he walked across the bridge to join his brothers for a delicious meal.

The three Billy Goats Gruff lived happily ever after and were never **concerned** about the mean troll again!

Respond to the Story

Retell: Use the prompts on the back of the Retelling Cards to help children retell the story.

Think About It

1. Who is the hero of this story? How did that character save the day?

2. Pretend you are the troll. What would you say to the Billy Goats at the end of the story?

Activity: Discuss with children the different sizes of the Billy Goats. Invite them to observe things in the classroom that are big, medium, and little. Then have each child fold a piece of paper into three sections and draw a little thing, a medium thing, and a big thing.

Listening Comprehension

Is Big Billy Goat afraid of the troll? How do you know?

The Three Little Pigs

A Tale from England

WONDERFUL WORD

delighted
Define: *Delighted* means very happy.
Example: Jane was *delighted* to see her friends at the park.
Ask: What makes you feel *delighted*?

Listening Comprehension

How are the three houses different from one another? Which one do you think would be the safest?

Once upon a time there were three little pigs who decided it was time to make their own way in the world. Each little pig set off to make a good house in which to live.

As the first little pig trotted along the road, he saw a pile of straw. "I will make my house from this nice straw," said the little pig. The little pig got to work and built himself a comfortable house.

The next little pig soon found a bundle of sticks. "I will use these nice sticks to make my house," said the little pig. The little pig got to work and built herself a beautiful house.

Then the next little pig went on his way and was **delighted** to come across a load of bricks. "These bricks will be perfect for my house," said the little pig. The little pig got to work and built himself a strong house.

Soon after the three houses were finished, a hungry wolf passed by the house of straw. First, he looked at the house, and then he smelled the little pig inside.

So he knocked on the door and said, "Little pig! Little pig! Let me in!"

But the little pig saw the wolf's big paws through the keyhole, so he answered back, "No! No! No! Not by the hair of my chinny chin chin!"

Then the wolf showed his teeth and said, "Then I'll huff and I'll puff and I'll blow your house in."

So he huffed and he puffed and he blew the house in. But the little pig was not there. He had run all the way to his sister's house of sticks.

As the wolf was very hungry, and could smell pigs from far away, he went straight to the house of sticks. He knocked on the door and said, "Little pigs! Little pigs! Let me in!"

But one little pig **peeked** through the keyhole, and the other peeked under the door. One saw the wolf's big ears, and the other saw his long tail. And they both answered back in the same breath, "No! No! No! Not by the hair of our chinny chin chins!"

Then the wolf showed his teeth and said, "Then I'll huff and I'll puff and I'll blow your house in."

So he huffed and he puffed and he blew the house in. But the wolf did not get the two little pigs, for they ran away as fast as they could and went straight to the little pig that lived in the house of bricks.

WONDERFUL WORD

peeked
Define: *Peeked* means looked quickly.
Example: I *peeked* through the window.
Ask: Have you ever *peeked* at your presents before your birthday?

Listening Comprehension

Why do you think the wolf shows his teeth?

furious

Define: *Furious* means very angry.
Example: Sarah was *furious* when her team lost the game.
Ask: What makes you feel *furious*?

Listening Comprehension

How do you think the wolf feels when he's trying to blow down the brick house? Act it out.

The hungry wolf went right after the little pigs. When he got to the house of bricks, he was very angry. He knocked hard on the door and said, "Little pigs! Little pigs! Let me in!"

But the three little pigs answered right back and said, "No! No! No! Not by the hair of our chinny chin chins!"

"Then I'll huff and I'll puff and I'll blow your house in," said the wolf, showing his teeth.

He huffed and he puffed. He puffed and he huffed. And he huffed, huffed, and he puffed, puffed; but the brick house was so strong that he could not blow it in.

The wolf was **furious** and said he would come down the chimney. But while he was climbing onto the roof, the little pigs made a blazing fire. When the wolf started to come down, he felt the hot flames. He quickly hopped out of the chimney and ran away from the three little pigs as fast as he could. And the three little pigs lived happily ever after!

Respond to the Story

Retell: Use the prompts on the back of the Retelling Cards to help children retell the story.

Think About It

1. How did the pigs help each other?

2. If the first two pigs were to rebuild their houses, what material do you think they would use? Why?

Activity: Invite children to build their favorite pig's house. Have them use paper or drinking straws for the straw house, craft sticks for the wood house, and clay for the brick house. Discuss how strong the houses are.

Tikki Tikki Tembo

A Tale from China

Long ago, in a small village in China, lived two small brothers. When the first brother was born, his parents had so many favorite names that they couldn't make up their minds. So they called him Tikki Tikki Tembo Nosarembo Merry Berry Tip Top Silly Billy Flip Flop Bush Berry Bembo. When the second brother was born, his parents had only one favorite name left. So they called him Chen.

Soon, the two little boys were big enough to play outside. Every day their mother warned them, "Do not go near the well, my little darlings, or one of these days you are **certain** to fall in."

One day, the brothers were chasing a kite when sure enough, Chen fell into the well. Down, down, down he went. Then splash! He hit the bottom of the well.

Tikki Tikki Tembo Nosarembo Merry Berry Tip Top Silly Billy Flip Flop Bush Berry Bembo ran to tell his mother. "Mother, Mother!" he cried. "Chen has fallen into the well!"

"What!" cried his mother. "I can hardly believe my ears. Tell me again."

WONDERFUL WORD

rescue

Define: To *rescue* is to save from danger.
Example: Firefighters *rescue* people from burning buildings.
Ask: How would you *rescue* a cat stuck in a tree?

Listening Comprehension

Why is the housepainter a good person to help rescue Chen from the well?

"Mother, Mother!" he repeated. "Chen has fallen into the well!"

"Oh, dear," cried his mother. "Our darling Chen has fallen into the well! We must **rescue** him. Go get the housepainter and tell him to bring his long ladder."

So Tikki Tikki Tembo Nosarembo Merry Berry Tip Top Silly Billy Flip Flop Bush Berry Bembo ran to the village. He found the housepainter, who was working on top of his long ladder.

"Oh, Honorable Housepainter," he said. "Chen has fallen into the well. Only your ladder can save him."

"Chen has fallen into the well!" cried the housepainter. "We must go help him at once!"

They ran to the well. The housepainter climbed down his ladder. Then he came back up the ladder, this time carrying Chen. Water came out of Chen's mouth. It came out of his nose. It even came out of his ears. But soon Chen was feeling better and all was well.

For a long time, the brothers did not play near the well.

But one day Tikki Tikki Tembo Nosarembo Merry Berry Tip Top Silly Billy Flip Flop Bush Berry Bembo ran to catch a ball. He jumped high in the air and fell right into the well. Down, down, down he went. Then splash! He hit the bottom of the well.

Chen ran to tell his mother. "Mother, Mother!" he cried. "Tikki Tikki Tembo Nosarembo Merry Berry Tip Top Silly Billy Flip Flop Bush Berry Bembo has fallen into the well!"

"What!" cried his mother. "I can hardly believe my ears. Tell me again."

"Mother," cried Chen, his voice shaking, "Tikki Tikki Tembo Nosarembo . . . Merry . . . Flop . . . bo . . ." But Chen was so shook up that he couldn't get another word out.

"Child, do you not know your own brother's name?" asked his mother. "For shame! Start again."

Chen took a big breath. "Mother!" he cried. "Tikki Tikki Tembo Nosarembo . . . Flip . . . Top. . ."

"Start again slowly," ordered his mother.

"Mother!" cried Chen. "Tikki Tikki Tembo Nosarembo Merry Berry Tip Top Silly Billy Flip Flop Bush Berry Bembo has fallen into the well!"

"Oh, dear!" cried his mother. "Tikki Tikki Tembo Nosarembo Merry Berry Tip Top Silly Billy Flip Flop Bush Berry Bembo has fallen into the well. We must rescue him! Quick, fetch the housepainter and tell him to bring his long ladder." So Chen ran to the village to get the housepainter.

"Oh, Honorable Housepainter," he cried, "Tikki Tikki . . . Merry . . . Berry." Chen stopped. He took a breath. He started again.

"Oh, Honorable Housepainter," he cried. "Tikki Tikki Tembo . . . Bush . . . Flip . . . Flop." Chen stopped. Tears started to roll down his cheeks.

"Boy, what are you trying to tell me?" asked the housepainter.

But by this time Chen was crying even harder. He cried and cried and then he sniffed. He took a breath and then he stood up tall. He closed his eyes so that he could **concentrate**.

Listening Comprehension

Why does Chen have a harder time getting help than his brother did?

WONDERFUL WORD

concentrate

Define: *Concentrate* means really pay attention to something.

Example: When I draw, I *concentrate* on what I am making.

Ask: What activities do you *concentrate* on?

Listening Comprehension

Why do Tikki Tikki Tembo's parents decide never to use his full name again?

"Oh, Honorable Housepainter," he cried. "Tikki Tikki Tembo Nosarembo Merry Berry Tip Top Silly Billy Flip Flop Bush Berry Bembo has fallen into the well!"

"What!" cried the housepainter. "Tikki Tikki Tembo Nosarembo Merry Berry Tip Top Silly Billy Flip Flop Bush Berry Bembo has fallen into the well! We must help him. Let's go!"

They ran to the well. The housepainter used his ladder to climb down to the bottom. Soon, he came up carrying Tikki Tikki Tembo Nosarembo Merry Berry Tip Top Silly Billy Flip Flop Bush Berry Bembo. Water came out of the boy's mouth. It came out of his nose. It came out of his ears. And it kept on coming.

Because of his long name, the boy had been in the water much longer than had his brother, Chen. And for a long time no one knew if he would be himself again. They brought him to his bed. By the time he opened his eyes wanting to play, several hours later, his parents had vowed to call him only by his first three names forever after.

And he was known as Tikki Tikki Tembo for the rest of his days.

Respond to the Story

Retell: Use the prompts on the back of the Retelling Cards to help children retell the story.

Think About It

1. Do you think this story is meant to be funny? What are some funny parts?

2. If this story happened in real life, would people know who Chen was talking about? What else in this story would probably be different in real life?

Activity: Have children make up their own long and silly names. Work with each child to write at least the first few syllables of the new name. Invite them to introduce themselves to the class using their new names and to call each other by their new names for the rest of the day. You may want to have the class decide on shortened versions such as Tikki Tikki Tembo.

TIMIMOTO

A Tale from Japan

Once upon a time in Japan, there lived an old man and an old woman. They were very lonely because they had no children. One day the old woman said to her husband, "I wish we had a child. I would like a little boy, even if he is no bigger than my finger."

On that very day, as the old woman went to fetch water, she heard crying by the side of the path. She looked in the grass and there lay a tiny baby, only one inch long, wrapped in a red handkerchief.

The old woman was overjoyed. She took the baby home and showed him to her husband. The old man fell in love with the baby immediately. They named him Timimoto.

Timimoto grew up, but not very much. When he was five years old, he was as tall as his mother's thumb. At fifteen, he was only as tall as his mother's middle finger.

One morning Timimoto said, "I am going on a **journey** to see the world. Do not worry about me, for I will return safely!"

His parents were sad but they did not want to stop him. They knew he would not be happy unless they let him go.

"You will need a sword," said his mother.

She took a sewing needle, slid it into a piece of straw, and tied it to his belt.

"Use this to defend yourself against danger," she said.

His father got a rice bowl from the cupboard and carried it down to the river. He gave a chopstick to his son and said, "Now you have a boat and a paddle."

Listening Comprehension

How is Timimoto different from other children? How do his parents feel about his size?

WONDERFUL WORD

journey
Define: A *journey* is a long trip.
Example: Annie's dream is to go on a *journey* around the world.
Ask: Have you ever been on a *journey*? Where did you go?

warned

Define: *Warned* means told about danger or a bad thing that might happen.

Example: Carmen's mom *warned* that she might get splinters if she walked barefoot.

Ask: What is something that you have been *warned* about?

Listening Comprehension

What is Timimoto's personality like? How can you tell?

Timimoto climbed into his boat. His parents **warned**, "Be safe, and remember to keep your distance from the night giant who lives on the other side of the river!" Then they said good-bye, and Timimoto paddled down the river.

It was not easy being a tiny boy in a rice bowl, all alone in the middle of a big river. But Timimoto was strong and brave, and he did not give up.

Timimoto was paddling along when he felt something slap him across his back. Turning quickly, he saw a huge green frog behind his boat. The frog's long tongue lashed out at him again.

Timimoto ducked. He pushed the chopstick as hard as he could against the giant frog's jaws. The frog tumbled over in the water and dived out of sight. Timimoto turned his boat and paddled across the river.

As the wind blew stronger, the waves got higher and higher. One wave broke over the bowl and almost turned it upside down. Timimoto paddled as hard as he could.

Finally he came to a dock on the riverbank, and climbed out of his boat. He saw a crowd of people running. Timimoto ran with them, though he didn't know why they were running. He hopped onto a cart to avoid being crushed. When the cart stopped, he jumped down.

"Thank you," he called up to the driver.

The driver looked all around and then he looked down at his feet.

"Ho, little one, you must be new in town," he said. "Don't you know that a terrible giant comes when the sun sets?"

Timimoto remembered his parents' warning and realized that the driver must be speaking about the night giant!

Soon all of the people went into their houses and the streets were empty. The sun went down. Timimoto heard the earth rumble. He looked up and saw a huge giant standing over him. Strong fingers closed around him and lifted him into the air.

"Ah-Ha! A tender little morsel!" roared the giant.

He popped Timimoto into his mouth. Timimoto drew his sword and stabbed the giant's tongue.

"AHHHHHH!" screamed the giant, and Timimoto leaped from his open mouth to the ground. The giant ran into the forest, crying out that he would never return. Timimoto heard cheering all around him. People poured from their houses into the street.

"You have **defeated** the giant!" they shouted.

All night long the people feasted and danced in Timimoto's honor. Then the sun came up and everyone went down to the dock. At last, Timimoto climbed into his little boat and headed home.

Listening Comprehension

Why do you think Timimoto doesn't hide like everyone else when he hears that the giant is coming?

WONDERFUL WORD

defeated

Define: To *defeat* someone is to beat that person in a battle or competition.
Example: Our soccer team *defeated* the best team in the league, so now we are the champions!
Ask: Have you ever been on a team that was *defeated*? How did you feel?

Respond to the Story

Retell: Use the prompts on the back of the Retelling Cards to help children retell the story.

Think About It

1. Why do you think Timimoto wanted to see the world?

2. How did Timimoto's size help him beat the giant?

Activity: Discuss with children the kinds of things they could do if they were as small as Timimoto. Invite them to draw pictures showing what they would do, and dictate sentences describing the pictures.

The Tortoise and the Hare

A Fable by Aesop

WONDERFUL WORD

boast

Define: To *boast* is to brag or speak very highly about yourself.
Example: My sister likes to *boast* that she is a great swimmer.
Ask: What have you heard someone *boast* about?

Listening Comprehension

Which animal can run faster, the tortoise or the hare? Who do you think will win the race?

A long time ago, there lived a tortoise and a hare. The tortoise spoke softly and was a bit shy, but the hare liked to **boast** about himself. One day the hare was boasting to the other animals in the forest about how fast he could run. "No one can run as fast as I can!" he said. "I dare anyone in the forest to race with me!"

The tortoise answered, "I will race with you." All the animals were amazed, for they knew that the tortoise was a very slow animal.

The hare, too, could hardly believe his ears. After he stopped laughing, he said, "But you are such a slowpoke! I can beat you without even trying!"

"We will see," said the tortoise in a soft voice. And the two decided to have a race the very next morning.

The next morning there was much excitement. All the big and little animals of the forest had gathered to watch the race. They were tired of hearing the hare brag. They all wanted the tortoise to win, but they didn't think he had a chance against the hare.

The second the race started, the hare leaped forward and was off! Soon he was out of sight. "I told you I was faster than you!" the hare called back to the tortoise. Then he laughed and laughed.

But the tortoise paid no attention to the hare. He just plodded on slowly and steadily.

The hare was way ahead in the race. When he looked back, he could hardly see the tortoise.

"I said I was the fastest animal in the forest," the hare declared. "Now the tortoise will find out that it is true!"

The hare felt so **confident** that he was going to win the race that he decided to take a little snooze. After all, it was such a beautiful day, and the sun felt so nice and warm. So the hare stretched out and fell asleep.

Meanwhile the tortoise continued to walk slowly but surely along the road. In fact he soon walked right past the hare, who was still fast asleep! Quietly the tortoise walked on, getting closer and closer to the finish line, where all the forest animals were cheering for him.

Then, just as the tortoise was about to cross the line, the hare woke up. "This can't be happening!" he shouted. "I am the fastest animal in the forest!" The hare began to sprint toward the finish line, but it was much too late for him to catch up. And so the tortoise slowly but surely won the race!

WONDERFUL WORD

confident
Define: *Confident* means sure or certain.
Example: I feel *confident* that I can write my name.
Ask: What do you feel *confident* about?

Listening Comprehension

Why does the hare decide to take a nap? Do you think that was a wise thing to do?

Respond to the Story

Retell: Use the prompts on the back of the Retelling Cards to help children retell the story.

Think About It

1. How are the personalities of the tortoise and the hare different?

2. What do you think the other animals in the forest said to the tortoise after he won the race?

Activity: Ask children which character they would root for in the race, the tortoise or the hare. Help them make encouraging signs to hold up on the sidelines. Children can draw pictures and/or dictate encouraging phrases such as, "Go, Tortoise!" or "Run, Hare!" Then reread the story and have children hold up their signs during the race.

The Turtle and the Flute

A Tale from Brazil

WONDERFUL WORD

joyful

Define: *Joyful* means very happy.

Example: The Browns are a very *joyful* family. They love to have fun.

Ask: What makes you feel *joyful*?

Listening Comprehension

Why does Turtle get worried when she hears the words "turtle soup"?

Long ago, on the banks of the Amazon River, a talented little turtle played her flute all day. She played **joyful** music that made all the birds and animals sway and hum. Turtle also loved to dance to the music as she played.

One day, after she had played and danced for hours, Turtle hid inside her shell with her flute and went to sleep. Soon after, a man saw Turtle sleeping on the riverbank. He picked her up and said, "Yum! Turtle soup will make a fine treat for dinner tonight."

The man carried Turtle home and put her in a cage. He closed the lid and put the cage in the yard.

"Don't let the turtle out of the cage," he said to his children. "Tonight we will have turtle soup."

Then the man went to work in the fields. The children stayed home and played in the yard.

When Turtle woke up, she was surprised and frightened to find herself in a cage. She bristled when she heard the children mention turtle soup. "I must get away!" she said to herself. She tried to open the cage but could not. Then she had an idea.

Turtle began to play her flute. She played the most spirited music that she knew. The children stopped their game and listened.

"Turtle is playing the flute!" they shouted.

"I can dance as well as play," called Turtle. "I can even play and dance at the same time. If you open the cage, you can watch me."

The children opened the cage, and Turtle started to dance. Turtle's shell banged against the sides of the cage as she danced.

The children laughed and clapped.

Turtle danced for a while, and then she stopped.

"I am stiff from dancing in this little cage," she said. "I need to stretch my legs. Let me go for a short walk. Then I can dance some more for you."

The children wanted Turtle to **entertain** them some more, so they let her out of the cage.

"Don't go far," they said.

WONDERFUL WORD

returned

Define: *Returned* means came back.

Example: I'm so tired because I just *returned* from my trip last night.

Ask: What time do you *return* home from school each day?

Turtle walked around and around the yard. She walked closer and closer to the forest. Then she crawled under some leaves and disappeared.

The children looked and looked for Turtle. "Turtle! Turtle!" they called. "Where are you?"

But there was no answer.

"Turtle tricked us!" they said.

When the children's father **returned** home from the fields, he too looked around the yard for Turtle. But it was too late. By that time, Turtle was sitting on the banks of the river once more, playing happy tunes on her flute.

Respond to the Story

Retell: Use the prompts on the back of the Retelling Cards to help children retell the story.

Think About It

1. How did Turtle use her flute to help her get free?

2. Explain how Turtle was more clever than the children.

Activity: Ask children to imagine what Turtle's music sounds like. Then have them work with partners to "write" or hum Turtle's song, with or without words.

THE VOICE IN RABBIT'S HOUSE

A Masai Tale

One day, while Rabbit was out, Caterpillar crawled inside Rabbit's house. When Rabbit came home, he noticed unfamiliar tracks in the dirt by the door.

"Who has entered my house?" Rabbit wondered. He peeked through the window, but saw nothing. He was too afraid to go inside.

"Hellooo!" Rabbit hollered. "Who's in my house?"

A deep, booming voice replied, "IT IS I, THE MOST POWERFUL AND TERRIBLE CREATURE IN THE LAND. I MAKE RHINOCEROS **TREMBLE** AND ELEPHANT HIDE IN FEAR."

"Such a creature would surely eat a little rabbit like me for dinner! What shall I do?" thought Rabbit. He ran to find help.

"Leopard, I need your help!" cried Rabbit. "There's a monster in my house!"

Leopard was not afraid. He stood by the window and growled, "Who is in Rabbit's house?"

"IT IS I, THE MOST POWERFUL AND TERRIBLE CREATURE IN THE LAND. I MAKE RHINOCEROS TREMBLE AND ELEPHANT HIDE IN FEAR." The caterpillar's voice shook Rabbit's house like an earthquake.

"I'm leaving!" screamed Leopard. "If this creature frightens Rhinoceros and Elephant, imagine what he could do to me!" And Leopard ran away.

"Oh, dear!" said Rabbit. He was very worried. He went to find Rhinoceros, to see if she could help.

"Rhinoceros, there is a terrible monster in my house!" said Rabbit. "Please help get him out!"

"There is no monster more terrible than I!" proclaimed Rhinoceros. Then she bellowed, "Who is in Rabbit's house?"

WONDERFUL WORD

tremble
Define: To *tremble* is to shake, especially from fear or excitement.
Example: The sound of thunder made Ana *tremble*.
Ask: What might make you *tremble*?

Listening Comprehension

What kind of creature does Rabbit think is in his house? What gives him that idea? Who is really in Rabbit's house?

Listening Comprehension

Why does Rhinoceros run away? What does she think is happening?

WONDERFUL WORD

agreed

Define: *Agreed* means said yes or thought the same thing as someone else.

Example: Aleesha *agreed* to help Joanie build a block tower.

Ask: What is something that you *agreed* to do?

"IT IS I, THE MOST POWERFUL AND TERRIBLE CREATURE IN THE LAND," said the caterpillar in his thunderous voice. "I MAKE RHINOCEROS TREMBLE AND ELEPHANT HIDE IN FEAR."

The caterpillar's voice was so loud that the ground beneath Rhinoceros's feet trembled. "I *AM* trembling!" said Rhinoceros. "What the creature says is true, which means he must be terrible, indeed!" She ran away, leaving Rabbit alone.

"Oh, dear!" cried Rabbit. He was very frustrated. "Perhaps Elephant can get the monster out of my house!" Rabbit found Elephant and begged him to help.

Elephant **agreed**. He pushed his trunk inside Rabbit's door and demanded, "Who is in Rabbit's house?"

"IT IS I, THE MOST POWERFUL AND TERRIBLE CREATURE IN THE LAND. I MAKE RHINOCEROS TREMBLE AND ELEPHANT HIDE IN FEAR." The caterpillar's mighty voice made the pebbles roll between Elephant's feet.

"Is it true?" Elephant asked Rabbit. "Did Rhinoceros really tremble?"

"She did tremble," answered Rabbit. "And then she ran away!"

"Rhinoceros is very fierce. If she trembled in fear of this creature, then I, too, must go and hide. Good-bye!" Elephant ran away and hid.

"Oh, dear!" cried Rabbit. "This is hopeless! I'll never get the monster out of my house! What will I ever do?"

Just then Frog passed by Rabbit's house. She heard Rabbit worrying. "Can *I* help you with something, Rabbit?" asked Frog.

"I doubt it," said Rabbit. "There is a terribly frightful monster in my house. Leopard, Rhinoceros, and Elephant each tried to help, and all of them ran away in fear. How could a small frog like you make the monster leave?"

"Let me try, anyway," said Frog.

Frog hopped to Rabbit's door and shouted in the biggest voice she could muster, "WHO IS IN RABBIT'S HOUSE?"

"IT IS I," replied Caterpillar in his giant voice, "THE MOST POWERFUL AND TERRIBLE CREATURE IN THE LAND. I MAKE RHINOCEROS TREMBLE AND ELEPHANT HIDE IN FEAR."

Frog hopped inside the house and replied, "I AM THE STRONGEST, MOST POWERFUL, AND MOST TERRIBLE CREATURE OF ALL. I FRIGHTEN THE CREATURE WHO CAUSES RHINOCEROS TO TREMBLE AND ELEPHANT TO HIDE IN FEAR. I **INSIST** THAT YOU LEAVE!"

When Caterpillar heard this, he started to shake. After all, he was only a small caterpillar, and a creature of such great strength could easily crush him. He decided to leave Rabbit's house at once. He slithered under a wall, trying not to be noticed.

But Rabbit spotted Caterpillar. "IT WAS YOU?" Rabbit shouted. He could not believe that the giant voice in his house had come from such a tiny caterpillar.

Rabbit turned to Frog and said, "Thank you so much! You saved me from quite a mighty creature!" They looked at the caterpillar and laughed.

Then Leopard, Rhinoceros, and Elephant all chuckled at the sight of the tiny caterpillar who had caused them such a fright.

WONDERFUL WORD

insist

Define: To *insist* on something is to demand it very firmly.
Example: My teacher *insists* that we clean up after playing.
Ask: What might you *insist* that a pet dog do?

Listening Comprehension

Why is Caterpillar more afraid of Frog than of the other animals?

Respond to the Story

Retell: Use the prompts on the back of the Retelling Cards to help children retell the story.

Think About It

1. How do you think Rabbit felt after he discovered who was in his house?

2. Can you think of any small animals that have loud voices? What do they use their loud voices for?

Activity: Have children make paper plate masks of their favorite characters from the story. Distribute paper plates and provide craft materials, such as yarn and buttons, for creating features. Then invite children to act out the story. Remind them to pay attention to their characters' voices.

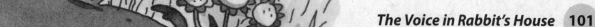

Mother Goose Rhymes

Mother Goose rhymes have been an important part of childhood for generations. These rhymes are among the most unchanging and universal parts of our literary heritage. The irresistible catchiness of their rhythms and the immediacy of their imagery make them easy to learn and impossible to forget. The cast of characters—from Jack and Jill and Old Mother Hubbard to Humpty Dumpty and Little Miss Muffet—are figures we meet again and again in all forms of popular culture.

Nursery rhymes are part of the oral tradition, and many go back for centuries. In the 18th century, several collections of nursery rhymes were printed under the name Mother Goose. Mother Goose is not an author or a pseudonym, but a figure who has come to represent the idea of the storyteller. No one knows the exact origin of the rhymes that are now part of most Mother Goose collections, but it is believed that many originated as children's games and puzzles, lullabies, and other forms of traditional amusement.

Using Mother Goose Rhymes in the Classroom

Mother Goose rhymes have many uses in the classroom. Their brevity is perfectly suited to the attention spans of young children. Their rich language, strong rhythms, and memorable characters and situations make them fun to listen to and easy to integrate into many parts of the curriculum.

The Mother Goose Puppet will draw children into the experience of listening to and reciting nursery rhymes. The puppet can be used to read the rhymes aloud, to help focus children on particular features of the rhymes, or to narrate retellings of the stories in the rhymes.

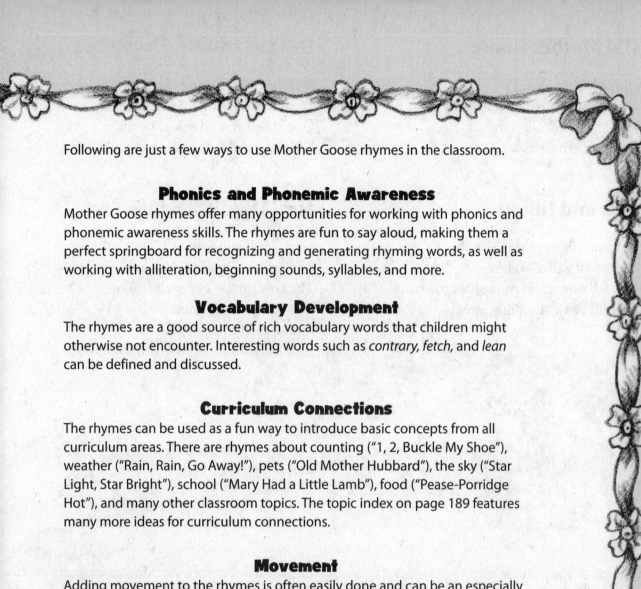

Following are just a few ways to use Mother Goose rhymes in the classroom.

Phonics and Phonemic Awareness

Mother Goose rhymes offer many opportunities for working with phonics and phonemic awareness skills. The rhymes are fun to say aloud, making them a perfect springboard for recognizing and generating rhyming words, as well as working with alliteration, beginning sounds, syllables, and more.

Vocabulary Development

The rhymes are a good source of rich vocabulary words that children might otherwise not encounter. Interesting words such as *contrary*, *fetch*, and *lean* can be defined and discussed.

Curriculum Connections

The rhymes can be used as a fun way to introduce basic concepts from all curriculum areas. There are rhymes about counting ("1, 2, Buckle My Shoe"), weather ("Rain, Rain, Go Away!"), pets ("Old Mother Hubbard"), the sky ("Star Light, Star Bright"), school ("Mary Had a Little Lamb"), food ("Pease-Porridge Hot"), and many other classroom topics. The topic index on page 189 features many more ideas for curriculum connections.

Movement

Adding movement to the rhymes is often easily done and can be an especially fun way to learn them. Some rhymes suggest movements in the main action (such as jumping over a candlestick), while other rhymes name body parts that children can point to or animals that can be imitated. There are many possibilities for improvisational movements in connection with the rhymes. Children love to learn these movements and to create them on their own.

Old Mother Goose

Old Mother Goose,
When she wanted to wander,
Would ride through the air
On a very fine gander.

Diddle, Diddle, Dumpling

Diddle, diddle, dumpling, my son John
Went to bed with his stockings on;
One shoe off, and one shoe on,
Diddle, diddle, dumpling, my son John.

Jack and Jill

Jack and Jill went up the hill
To fetch a pail of water.
Jack fell down and broke his crown,
And Jill came tumbling after.

Hey! Diddle, Diddle

Hey! diddle, diddle,
The cat and the fiddle,
The cow jumped over the moon;
The little dog laughed
To see such a sport,
And the dish ran away with the spoon.

Six Little Mice

Six little mice sat down to spin;
Pussy passed by and she peeped in.
What are you doing, my little men?
Weaving coats for gentlemen.
Shall I come in and cut off your threads?
No, no, Mistress Pussy, you'd bite off our heads.
Oh, no, I'll not; I'll help you to spin.
That may be so, but you can't come in.

To Market

To market, to market, to buy a fat pig,
Home again, home again, jiggety jig.
To market, to market, to buy a fat hog,
Home again, home again, jiggety jog.
To market, to market, to buy a plum bun,
Home again, home again, market is done.

Pease-Porridge Hot

Pease-porridge hot,
Pease-porridge cold,
Pease-porridge in the pot,
Nine days old.
Some like it hot,
Some like it cold,
Some like it in the pot,
Nine days old.

Rain, Rain, Go Away

Rain, rain, go away.
Come again some other day.
Rain, rain, go away.
Little children want to play.

Three Little Kittens

Three little kittens,
They lost their mittens,
And they began to cry,
Oh, Mother dear,
We sadly fear
Our mittens we have lost.
What! Lost your mittens,
You naughty kittens!
Then you shall have no pie.
Mee-ow, mee-ow, mee-ow.
No, you shall have no pie.

The three little kittens,
They found their mittens,
And they began to cry,
Oh, Mother dear,
See here, see here,
Our mittens we have found.
Put on your mittens,
You silly kittens,
And you shall have some pie.
Purr-r, purr-r, purr-r,
Oh, let us have some pie.

The three little kittens
Put on their mittens
And soon ate up the pie;
Oh, Mother dear,
We greatly fear
Our mittens we have soiled.
What! Soiled your mittens,
You naughty kittens!
Then they began to sigh,
Mee-ow, mee-ow, mee-ow.
Then they began to sigh.

The three little kittens,
They washed their mittens,
And hung them out to dry;
Oh, Mother dear,
Do you not hear,
Our mittens we have washed.
What! Washed your mittens,
Then you're good kittens,
But I smell a rat close by.
Mee-ow, mee-ow, mee-ow,
We smell a rat close by.

The Pumpkin Eater

Peter, Peter, pumpkin eater,
Had a wife and couldn't keep her;
He put her in a pumpkin shell,
And there he kept her very well.

Doctor Foster

Doctor Foster went to Gloucester
In a shower of rain;
He stepped in a puddle,
Right up to his middle,
And never went there again.

The Crooked Man

There was a crooked man,
And he walked a crooked mile.
He found a crooked sixpence
Against a crooked stile;
He bought a crooked cat,
Which caught a crooked mouse,
And they all lived together
In a little crooked house.

If I Had a Donkey

If I had a donkey that wouldn't go,
Would I poke him? Oh no, no.
I'd put him in the barn and give him
    some corn.
The best little donkey that ever was born.

Jack Sprat

Jack Sprat could eat no fat.
His wife could eat no lean.
And so between them both, you see,
They licked the platter clean.

Wee Willie Winkie

Wee Willie Winkie runs through the town,
Upstairs and downstairs in his nightgown,
Rapping at the window, crying through the
    lock,
"Are the children in their beds, for now it's
    eight o'clock?"

Little Jack Horner

Little Jack Horner
Sat in a corner,
Eating his holiday pie.
He put in his thumb,
And pulled out a plum,
And said, "What a good boy am I!"

Polly Put the Kettle On

Polly put the kettle on,
Polly put the kettle on,
Polly put the kettle on,
We'll all have tea.

Sukey take it off again,
Sukey take it off again,
Sukey take it off again,
They've all gone away.

It's Raining

It's raining, it's pouring,
The old man is snoring;
He went to bed
And bumped his head
And couldn't get up in the morning.

Mary, Mary, Quite Contrary

Mary, Mary, quite contrary,
How does your garden grow?
With cockleshells, and silver bells,
And pretty maids all in a row.

Ride Away, Ride Away

Ride away, ride away,
Johnny shall ride,
And he shall have pussy-cat
Tied to one side;
And he shall have little dog
Tied to the other,
And Johnny shall ride
To see his grandmother.

My Black Hen

Higgledy, piggledy, my black hen,
She lays eggs for gentlemen;
Sometimes nine, sometimes ten;
Higgledy, piggledy, my black hen.

Blow, Wind, Blow!

Blow, wind, blow! And go, mill, go!
That the miller may grind his corn;
That the baker may take it,
And into rolls make it,
And send us some hot in the morn.

If All the World Was Paper

If all the world was paper,
And all the seas were ink,
If all the trees were bread and cheese,
What would we have to drink?

Star Light

Star light, star bright,
First star I see tonight,
I wish I may, I wish I might,
Have the wish I wish tonight.

Little Boy Blue

Little Boy Blue,
Come blow your horn.
The sheep's in the meadow,
The cow's in the corn.
Where is the boy
That looks after the sheep?
He's under a haystack
Fast asleep.
Will you wake him?
No, not I,
For if I do,
He's sure to cry.

Baa, Baa, Black Sheep

Baa, baa, black sheep,
Have you any wool?
Yes, sir, yes, sir,
Three bags full;
One for my master,
And one for my dame,
And one for the little boy
Who lives down the lane.

Tommy Tucker

Little Tommy Tucker
Sings for his supper.
What shall we give him?
White bread and butter.
How shall he cut it
Without e'er a knife?
How shall he marry
Without e'er a wife?

1, 2, Buckle My Shoe

One, two,
Buckle my shoe;
Three, four,
Shut the door;
Five, six,
Pick up sticks;
Seven, eight,
Lay them straight;
Nine, ten,
A big, fat hen.

If All the Seas

If all the seas were one sea,
What a great sea that would be!
If all the trees were one tree,
What a great tree that would be!
And if all the axes were one ax,
What a great ax that would be!
And if all the men were one man,
What a great man he would be!
And if the great man took the great ax,
And cut down the great tree,
And let it fall into the great sea,
What a splish-splash that would be!

Mary Had a Little Lamb

Mary had a little lamb,
Its fleece was white as snow;
And everywhere that Mary went
The lamb was sure to go.

It followed her to school one day,
That was against the rule;
It made the children laugh and play
To see a lamb at school.

1, 2, 3, 4, 5

One, two, three, four, five,
Once I caught a fish alive,
Six, seven, eight, nine, ten,
Then I let it go again.
Why did you let it go?
Because it bit my finger so.
Which finger did it bite?
The little finger on the right.

Roses Are Red

Roses are red,
Violets are blue,
Sugar is sweet
And so are you.

Little Bo-Peep

Little Bo-Peep has lost her sheep,
And can't tell where to find them;
Leave them alone, and they'll come home,
Wagging their tails behind them.

Peter Piper

Peter Piper picked a peck of pickled peppers;
A peck of pickled peppers Peter Piper picked;
If Peter Piper picked a peck of pickled
    peppers,
Where's the peck of pickled peppers Peter
    Piper picked?

Humpty Dumpty

Humpty Dumpty sat on a wall,
Humpty Dumpty had a great fall;
All the king's horses and
All the king's men
Couldn't put Humpty
Together again.

Old Woman

There was an old woman
Lived under a hill,
And if she's not gone
She lives there still.

Hoddley, Poddley

Hoddley, poddley, puddle and fogs,
Cats are to marry the poodle dogs;
Cats in blue jackets and dogs in red hats,
What will become of the mice and the rats?

Hickory, Dickory, Dock

Hickory, dickory, dock,
The mouse ran up the clock;
The clock struck one,
The mouse ran down;
Hickory, dickory, dock!

Pussy-Cat, Pussy-Cat

Pussy-cat, pussy-cat, where have you been?
"I've been to London to look at the queen."
Pussy-cat, pussy-cat, what did you do there?
"I frightened a little mouse under the chair."

Hot Cross Buns

Hot cross buns! Hot cross buns!
One a penny, two a penny,
Hot cross buns!
If you have no daughters,
Give them to your sons;
One a penny, two a penny,
Hot cross buns.

Pat-a-Cake

Pat-a-cake, pat-a-cake, baker's man,
Bake me a cake as fast as you can.
Pat it and prick it, and mark it with B,
And put it in the oven for Baby and me.

Tweedledum and Tweedledee

Tweedledum and Tweedledee
Agreed to have a battle,
For Tweedledum said Tweedledee
Had spoiled his nice new rattle.
Just then flew by a monstrous crow
As big as a tar-barrel,
Which frightened both the heroes so,
They quite forgot their quarrel.

Three Men in a Tub

Rub-a-dub-dub,
Three men in a tub,
And who do you think they be?
The butcher, the baker,
The candlestick maker,
All paddling out to sea.

The Pie

Who made the pie?
I did.
Who stole the pie?
He did.
Who found the pie?
You did.
Who cried for the pie?
We all did.

Sulkey Sue

Here's Sulkey Sue;
What shall we do?
Turn her face to the wall
Till she comes to.

Old Mother Hubbard

Old Mother Hubbard
Went to the cupboard
To fetch her poor dog a bone;
But when she got there,
The cupboard was bare,
And so the poor dog had none.

Little Miss Muffet

Little Miss Muffet
Sat on a tuffet,
Eating her curds and whey;
Along came a spider,
Who sat down beside her
And frightened Miss Muffet away.

Sing a Song of Sixpence

Sing a song of sixpence,
A pocket full of rye.
Four and twenty blackbirds
Baked in a pie.

When the pie was opened,
The birds began to sing.
Wasn't that a dainty dish
To set before the king?

The king was in his counting-house
Counting out his money.
The queen was in the parlor
Eating bread and honey.

The maid was in the garden
Hanging out the clothes,
When along came a blackbird
And pecked off her nose.

Tom, Tom, the Piper's Son

Tom, Tom, the piper's son,
Stole a pig and away he run;
The pig was eat, and Tom was beat,
And Tom went roaring down the street.

The North Wind

The north wind doth blow,
And we shall have snow,
And what will poor robin do then,
Poor thing?
He'll sit in a barn,
And keep himself warm,
And hide his head under his wing,
Poor thing.

Hush-a-Bye

Hush-a-bye, baby, on the treetop,
When the wind blows, the cradle will rock;
When the bough breaks, the cradle will
  fall;
Down will come baby, cradle and all.

Ring Around the Rosy

Ring around the rosy,
Pocket full of posy,
Ashes, ashes,
All fall down!

Higglety, Pigglety, Pop

Higglety, pigglety, pop!
The dog has eaten the mop.
The pig's in a hurry,
The cat's in a flurry,
Higglety, pigglety, pop!

The Owl

A wise old owl sat in an oak,
The more he heard, the less he spoke;
The less he spoke, the more he heard.
Why aren't we all like that wise old bird?

One Misty, Moisty Morning

One misty, moisty morning,
When cloudy was the weather,
I chanced to meet an old man
Clothed all in leather.

He began to compliment,
And I began to grin,
How do you do, and how do you do,
And how do you do again?

Simple Simon

Simple Simon met a pieman
Going to the fair;
Says Simple Simon to the pieman,
"Let me taste your ware."

Says the pieman to Simple Simon,
"Show me first your penny."
Says Simple Simon to the pieman,
"Indeed, I have not any."

Simple Simon went a-fishing
For to catch a whale,
All the water he had got
Was in his mother's pail!

Ding, Dong, Bell

Ding, dong, bell,
Pussy's in the well.
Who put her in?
Little Johnny Green.
Who pulled her out?
Little Tommy Stout.
What a naughty boy was that
To try to drown poor pussy-cat,
Who never did him any harm,
But killed the mice in his father's barn.

Jack-a-Nory

I'll tell you a story
About Jack-a-Nory,
And now my story's begun;
I'll tell you another
About Jack and his brother,
And now my story is done.

Georgy Porgy

Georgy Porgy, pudding and pie,
Kissed the girls and made them cry.
When the boys came out to play,
Georgy Porgy ran away.

The Bat

Bat, bat, come under my hat,
And I'll give you a slice of bacon;
And when I bake, I'll give you a cake,
If I am not mistaken.

The Old Woman
Who Lived in a Shoe

There was an old woman who lived in a shoe;
She had so many children she didn't know
    what to do.
She gave them some broth without any bread;
Then brushed their hair and put them to bed.

Jack, Be Nimble

Jack, be nimble,
Jack, be quick,
Jack, jump over
The candlestick.

Bow-Wow

Bow-wow says the dog,
Meow, meow says the cat,
Grunt, grunt goes the hog,
And squeak goes the rat.

Whoo-oo says the owl,
Caw, caw says the crow,
Quack, quack says the duck,
And what cuckoos say, you know.

So with cuckoos and owls,
With rats and dogs,
With ducks and with crows,
With cats and with hogs,

A fine song I have made,
To please you, my dear;
And if it's well-sung,
'Twill be charming to hear.

Three Blind Mice

Three blind mice, see how they run!
They all ran after the farmer's wife,
Who cut off their tails with a carving knife.
Did you ever see such a thing in your life,
As three blind mice?

Going to St. Ives

As I was going to St. Ives,
I met a man with seven wives.
Each wife had seven sacks,
Each sack had seven cats,
Each cat had seven kits.
Kits, cats, sacks, and wives,
How many were there going to St. Ives?

This Is the House That Jack Built

This is the house that Jack built.

This is the malt
That lay in the house that Jack built.

This is the rat,
That ate the malt
That lay in the house that Jack built.

This is the cat,
That killed the rat,
That ate the malt
That lay in the house that Jack built.

This is the dog,
That worried the cat,
That killed the rat,
That ate the malt
That lay in the house that Jack built.

This is the cow with the crumpled horn,
That tossed the dog,
That worried the cat,
That killed the rat,
That ate the malt
That lay in the house that Jack built.

This is the maiden all forlorn,
That milked the cow with the crumpled
   horn,
That tossed the dog,
That worried the cat,
That killed the rat,
That ate the malt
That lay in the house that Jack built.

This is the man all tattered and torn,
That kissed the maiden all forlorn,
That milked the cow with the crumpled
   horn,
That tossed the dog,
That worried the cat,
That killed the rat,
That ate the malt
That lay in the house that Jack built.

This is the priest all shaven and shorn,
That married the man all tattered and torn,
That kissed the maiden all forlorn,
That milked the cow with the crumpled
    horn,
That tossed the dog,
That worried the cat,
That killed the rat,
That ate the malt
That lay in the house that Jack built.

This is the cock that crowed in the morn,
That waked the priest all shaven and shorn,
That married the man all tattered and torn,
That kissed the maiden all forlorn,
That milked the cow with the crumpled
    horn,
That tossed the dog,
That worried the cat,
That killed the rat,
That ate the malt
That lay in the house that Jack built.

This is the farmer sowing his corn,
That kept the cock that crowed in the
    morn,
That waked the priest all shaven and shorn,
That married the man all tattered and torn,
That kissed the maiden all forlorn,
That milked the cow with the crumpled
    horn,
That tossed the dog,
That worried the cat,
That killed the rat,
That ate the malt
That lay in the house that Jack built.

Song Favorites

Children love to hear and sing songs. Music naturally engages children and can create wonderful opportunities for learning. A song can change the dynamic of the classroom by lifting children's spirits or calming them down.

The songs in this collection are old and new, and come from all around the world. Some of the songs tell stories. Others are delightful nonsense. Some are meant for celebrations, others for games, dancing, or going to bed. Some can be used to help children learn the alphabet, counting, or other skills. Others inspire wonder about the world around them.

Songs can develop children's literacy skills. They are a great tool for preparing children to read. They can be used to highlight structural elements that are also found in stories and poems, such as form, rhythm, and rhyme. In addition, songs inspire children to express themselves. Children often add their own verses to their favorite songs, or create entirely new songs about their experiences, in effect becoming writers.

Traditional songs bring children into contact with their musical and cultural heritages. Many were passed down orally from generation to generation. This is why there can be many versions of the same song. By learning to sing these songs, children learn about the people who came before us, and become aware of the central role that music plays in our lives.

Using Song Favorites in the Classroom

Songs can play an integral role in the classroom and can be used to support curriculum and other aspects of classroom life.

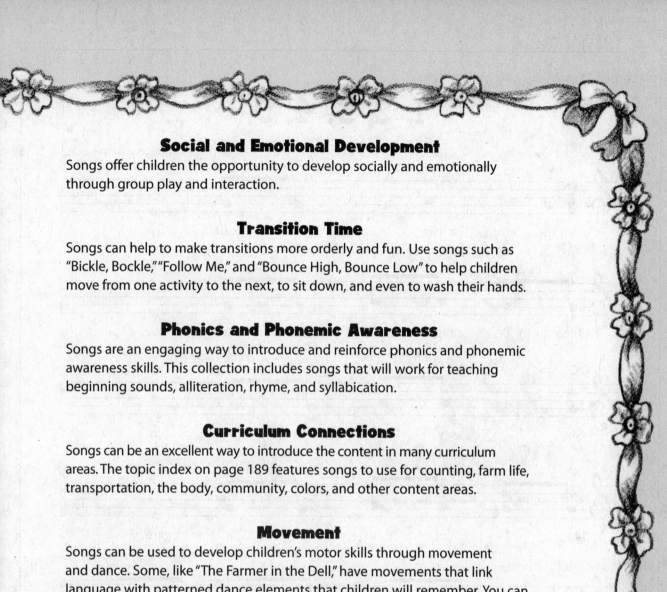

Social and Emotional Development

Songs offer children the opportunity to develop socially and emotionally through group play and interaction.

Transition Time

Songs can help to make transitions more orderly and fun. Use songs such as "Bickle, Bockle," "Follow Me," and "Bounce High, Bounce Low" to help children move from one activity to the next, to sit down, and even to wash their hands.

Phonics and Phonemic Awareness

Songs are an engaging way to introduce and reinforce phonics and phonemic awareness skills. This collection includes songs that will work for teaching beginning sounds, alliteration, rhyme, and syllabication.

Curriculum Connections

Songs can be an excellent way to introduce the content in many curriculum areas. The topic index on page 189 features songs to use for counting, farm life, transportation, the body, community, colors, and other content areas.

Movement

Songs can be used to develop children's motor skills through movement and dance. Some, like "The Farmer in the Dell," have movements that link language with patterned dance elements that children will remember. You can encourage children's creativity by having them create their own movements.

Performance

Music can serve as a perfect centerpiece for your family nights and other special occasions. Get parents involved by distributing song sheets or having them play rhythm instruments.

1, 2, 3, 4, 5

American Game Song

One, two, three, four, five,

Once I caught a fish a - live.

Six, sev - en, eight, nine, ten,

Then I let it go a - gain.

Solo 1
Why did you let it go? Be -
Which fin - ger did it bite? The

cause it bit my fin - ger so!
lit - tle fin - ger on the right!

Solo 2

1, 2, Buckle My Shoe

Traditional Rhyme

One, two, Buck-le my shoe; Three, four, Shut the door; Five, six,

Pick up sticks; Sev—en, eight, lay them straight; Nine, ten, a big fat hen.

A be ce

Latin American Folk Song
Adapted by Jenny Wells Vincent

Spanish: A be ce che de e e - fe ge___ ha - che i jo - ta
Pronunciation: a be se che ðe e ɛ fe xe a che i xo ta

ka e - le e - lle e - me e - ne e - ñe o pe cu
ka ɛ le ɛ ye ɛ me ɛ ne ɛ nye o pe ku

e - re e - rre e - se te u ve y do - ble ve
ɛ ɾe ɛ r̄e ɛ se te u βe i ðo ble βe

e - quis e i grie - ga con ze - ta ya a - ca - bé.
ɛ kis e i gɾye ga kon se ta ya ka βe

Pronunciation Guide: "A be ce"

ɑ f<u>a</u>ther	e <u>a</u>pe	ɛ p<u>e</u>t	i b<u>ee</u>
o <u>o</u>bey	u m<u>oo</u>n	β *b* without lips touching	
ð <u>th</u>e	ɾ flipped r	r̄ rolled r	
x slightly guttural h, *Spanish* ba<u>j</u>o			

Alphabet Song

Traditional

America

Music by Henry Carey
Words by Samuel F. Smith

My coun-try 'tis of thee, Sweet land of lib-er-ty,

Of thee I sing. Land where my fa-thers died,

Land of the Pil-grim's pride, From ev-'ry

moun-tain-side Let free-dom ring.

America, the Beautiful

Music by Samuel Ward
Words by Katharine Lee Bates

1. O beau - ti - ful for spa - cious skies, For am - ber waves of
2. O beau - ti - ful for he - roes proved In lib - er - at - ing
3. O beau - ti - ful for pa - triot dream That sees be - yond the

grain. For pur - ple moun - tain maj - es - ties A -
strife, Who more than self their coun - try loved, And
years, Thine al - a - bas - ter cit - ies gleam, Un -

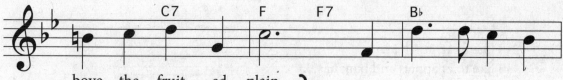

bove the fruit - ed plain.
mer - cy more than life.   A - mer - i - ca! A -
dim'd by hu - man tears.

mer - i - ca! God shed His grace on thee, And

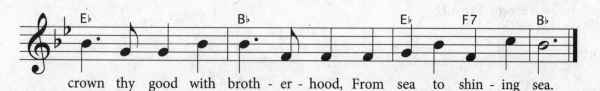

crown thy good with broth - er - hood, From sea to shin - ing sea.

Apples and Bananas

Traditional Children's Game

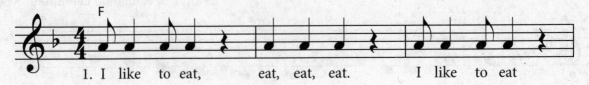

1. I like to eat, eat, eat, eat. I like to eat

ap - ples and ba - nan - as.___ I like to eat, eat, eat, eat.

I like to eat ap - ples and ba - nan - as.___

2. I like to āt, āt, āt, āt.
   I like to āt āpples and bānānās…

3. I like to ēt…ēpples and bēnēnēs…

4. I like to īt…īpples and bīnīnīs…

5. I like to ōt…ōpples and bōnōnōs…

6. I like to ūt…ūpples and būnūnūs…

(Repeat Verse 1)

Autumn Leaves

Anonymous

Au - tumn leaves are fall - ing, Nights are grow - ing chill.

Ma - ple leaves are turn-ing red a - long the hill.

Bell Horses

English Nursery Rhyme

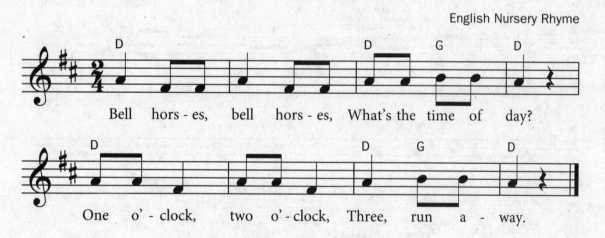

Bell hors - es, bell hors - es, What's the time of day?

One o' - clock, two o' - clock, Three, run a - way.

Bickle, Bockle

Traditional Singing Game

Bick-le, bock-le, blue bot-tle, fish-es in the sea.

1. If you want a part - ner, just choose me.
2. If your name be - gins with ___ then go line up.
3. If you're wear - ing ___ then sit at the ta–ble.

Bingo

Traditional Folk Song

There was a farm-er had a dog, and Bin-go was his name - O,

B - I - N - G - O,   B - I - N - G - O,

B - I - N - G - O, and Bing-o was his name - O.

2. ... (clap) - I - N - G - O ...
3. ... (clap) - (clap) - N - G - O ...
4. ... (clap) - (clap) - (clap) - G - O ...
5. ... (clap) - (clap) - (clap) - (clap) - O ...
6. ... (clap) - (clap) - (clap) - (clap) - (clap) ...

Bounce High, Bounce Low

Traditional
Verses 2–4 by MMH

1. Bounce high, bounce low, bounce the ball to Shi - loh!
2. Lis - ten, lis - ten, put your list' - ning ears on,
3. Qui - et, qui - et, qui - et like a mouse creeps,
4. Clean up, clean up, time to put your things a - way.

Bounce high, bounce low, bounce the ball to Shi - loh!
Lis - ten, list - en, all the noise should be gone! *(Shhhh)*
Qui - et, qui - et, al - most like you're fast a - sleep. *(Snore)*
Clean up, clean up, save them for an - oth—er day.

Burn, Little Candles

Hebrew Folk Song

1. Burn, lit-tle can-dles, burn, burn, burn. Burn-ing bright and clear.

Burn, lit-tle can-dles, burn, burn, burn. Ha-nuk-kah is here.

2. Eight little candles in a row,
   Hanukkah is here.
   Eight little candles in a row,
   Burn so bright and clear.

3. Dance, little candles, dance, dance, dance.
   Hanukkah is here.
   Dance, little candles, dance, dance, dance.
   Hanukkah is here.

Bye 'n' Bye

African American Spiritual

Stars shin-ing num — ber, num — ber {1. one,} {2. four,} num - ber

{1. two,} {2. five,} num-ber {1. three,} {2. six,} good Lord. Bye 'n' bye, bye 'n' bye, good

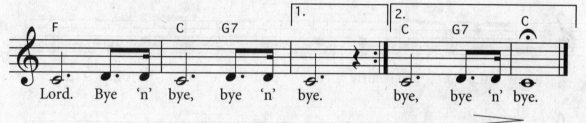

Lord. Bye 'n' bye, bye 'n' bye. bye, bye 'n' bye.

Clap Your Hands

American Folk Song

1. Clap, clap, clap your hands, Clap your hands to - geth - er,
2. Stamp, stamp, stamp your feet, Stamp them all to - geth - er,
3. Nod, nod, nod your heads, Nod them all to - geth - er,

Clap, clap, clap your hands, Clap your hands to - geth - er.
Stamp, stamp, stamp your feet, Stamp them all to - geth - er.
Nod, nod, nod your heads, Nod them all to - geth - er.

Down at the Station

Traditional

Down at the sta - tion, ear - ly in the morn - ing,

See the lit - tle puf - fer bil - lies all in a row.

See the en - gine driv - er pull the lit - tle han - dle.

Chug! Chug! Woo! Woo! Off we go.

Eency Weency Spider

Traditional Rhyme

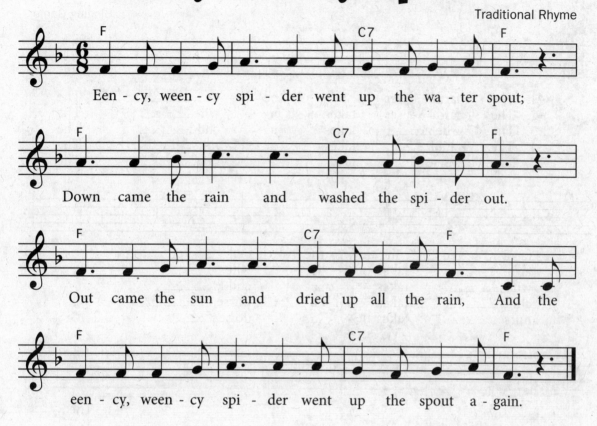

Een - cy, ween - cy spi - der went up the wa - ter spout;

Down came the rain and washed the spi - der out.

Out came the sun and dried up all the rain, And the

een - cy, ween - cy spi - der went up the spout a - gain.

Engine, Engine, Number Nine

American Song

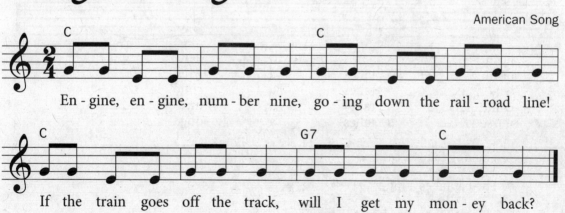

En - gine, en - gine, num - ber nine, go - ing down the rail - road line!

If the train goes off the track, will I get my mon - ey back?

The Farmer in the Dell

Singing Game

6. The dog takes a cat,...

7. The cat takes a rat,...

8. The rat takes the cheese,...

9. The cheese stands alone,...

Five Fat Turkeys

Traditional

Five fat tur - keys are we,_____ We

slept all night in a tree._____ When the

cook came a - round we could - n't be found, So

that's why we're here, you see._____

Follow Me

French Folk Melody
Verses 2–4 by MMH

1. Will you fol - low me in a line, in a line?
2. Will you fol - low me clean - ing up, clean-ing up?

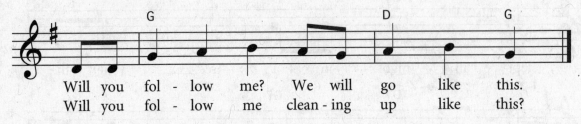

Will you fol - low me? We will go like this.
Will you fol - low me clean - ing up like this?

3. Will you follow me sitting down, sitting down?
   Will you follow me sitting down like this?

4. Will you follow me washing hands, washing hands?
   Will you follow me washing hands like this? *(Sing "Alphabet Song.")*

Go A Tin
(Lantern Song)

Taiwanese Folk Song
English Version by MMH

Taiwanese: 古 仔 燈   古 仔 燈
Pronunciation: go a tin   go a tin
English: Lan - tern bright, lan - tern bright,

大 家 來 提 古 仔 燈
dai ge lai gya go a tin
Light the___ way, my___ lan - tern bright.

Go Tell It on the Mountain

African American Spiritual

Swing Rhythm

Go, tell it on the moun - tain,

O - ver___ the hills and ev - 'ry - where.

Go, tell it on the moun - tain,

That Je - sus Christ___ is born.

Gogo

Kenyan Folk Song
As Sung by Mary Okari
English Words by Linda Worsley

Good Day Song

French Folk Song
Additional English Lyrics by MMH

1. When cats get up in the morn - ing, they
al - ways say good day.___ When cats get up in the
morn - ing, they al - ways say good day.___
"Meow, meow, meow, meow," That is what they say, they say.
"Meow, meow, meow, meow," That is what they say.___

2. dogs...bark (low)

3. cows...moo (low)

4. pigs...oink (high)

Hello Song

Singing Game

2. Stamp,…feet,…

3. Nod,…head,…

Higglety, Pigglety, Pop

Mother Goose Rhyme

1. Hig - gle - ty, Pig - gle - ty, pop! The
2. Dick - er - y, dick - er - y, dare, The

dog has eat - en the mop. The
pig flew up in the air. The

pig's in a hur - ry, The cat's in a flur - ry,
man___ in brown_____ Soon brought him down,___

Hig - gle - ty, Pig - gle - ty, pop!
Dick - er - y, dick - er - y, dare.

The Hokey Pokey

Words and Music by Charles P. Macak,
Taffy Baker and Larry LaPrise
American Singing Game

1. You put your right foot in, You put your
2. You put your left foot in, You put your

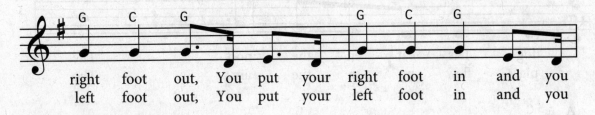

right foot out, You put your right foot in and you
left foot out, You put your left foot in and you

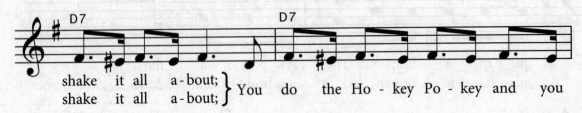

shake it all a-bout;
shake it all a-bout; } You do the Ho-key Po-key and you

turn your-self a-round. That's what it's all a-bout!

3. You put your right arm in,…

4. You put your left arm in,…

5. You put your whole self in,…

Hop, Hop, Hop

Children's Game Song

Up and down to earth and sky, Go my po - go stick and I,

Jog - ging, spring - ing, see me fly! Hop! Hop! Hop!

Hush, Little Baby

Southern U.S. Folk Song

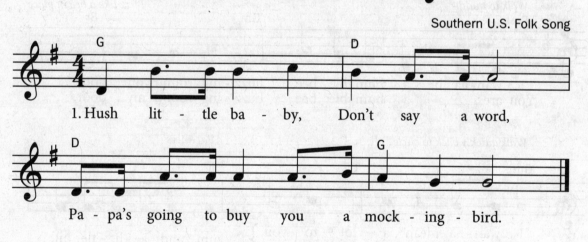

1. Hush lit - tle ba - by, Don't say a word,

Pa - pa's going to buy you a mock - ing - bird.

2. If that mockingbird won't sing,… diamond ring.

3. If that diamond ring turns brass, … looking glass.

4. If that looking glass gets broke, … billy goat.

5. If that billy goat's not smart,…horse and cart.

6. If that horse and cart fall down, You'll still be the sweetest baby in town.

I Wanna Be a Friend of Yours

American Singing Game

1. I wan-na be a friend of yours,
2. Oh, you__ are a friend of mine, } mmmm and a lit-tle bit more.

I wan-na be a pal of yours,
You are_____ a pal of mine, } mmmm and a lit-tle bit more.

I wan-na be a bum-ble bee buzz-ing round your door.
You are_____ a bum-ble bee buzz-ing round my door.

I wan-na mean a lot to you,
You mean_____ a lot to me, } mm and a lit-tle bit,

mm and a lit-tle bit, mm and a whole lot more!

If You're Happy

Singing Game

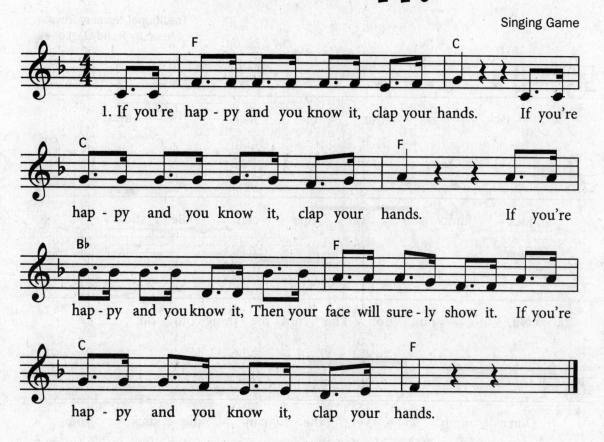

1. If you're hap - py and you know it, clap your hands. If you're

hap - py and you know it, clap your hands. If you're

hap - py and you know it, Then your face will sure - ly show it. If you're

hap - py and you know it, clap your hands.

2. If you're happy and you know it, tap your foot.

3. If you're happy and you know it, nod your head.

4. If you're happy and you know it, do all three.

Jack, Be Nimble

Traditional Nursery Rhyme
Music by Randy DeLelles

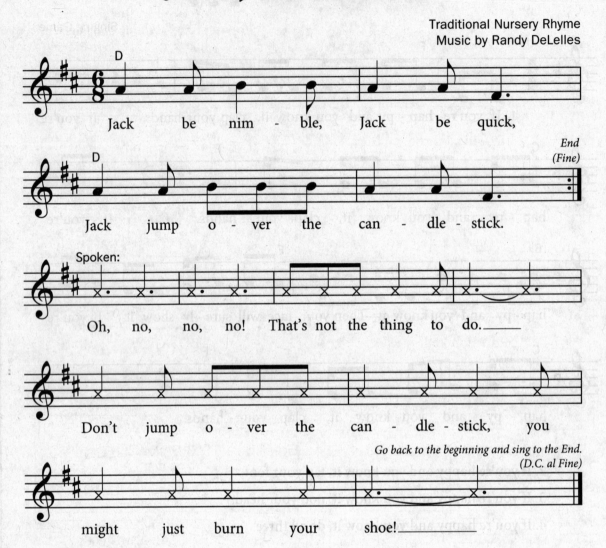

Jack be nim - ble, Jack be quick,

End (Fine)

Jack jump o - ver the can - dle - stick.

Spoken:

Oh, no, no, no! That's not the thing to do._____

Don't jump o - ver the can - dle - stick, you

Go back to the beginning and sing to the End.
(D.C. al Fine)

might just burn your shoe!_____

Jingle Bells

Words and Music by
James Pierpont

Dash - ing through the snow, In a one - horse o - pen sleigh,

O'er the fields we go, Laugh - ing all the way;

Bells on Bob - tail ring, Mak - ing spir - its bright, What

fun it is to ride and sing a sleigh - ing song to - night!

Jin - gle bells, jin - gle bells, jin - gle all the way! Oh, what fun it

is to ride in a one-horse o - pen sleigh!___ one-horse o - pen sleigh!

Kum Ba Yah

Traditional Gullah Song

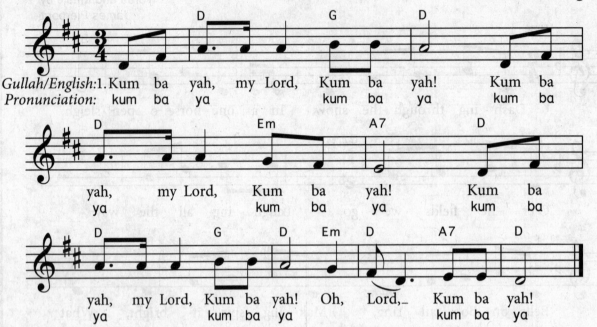

Gullah/English: 1. Kum ba yah, my Lord, Kum ba yah! Kum ba
Pronunciation: kum ba ya kum ba ya kum ba

yah, my Lord, Kum ba yah! Kum ba
ya kum ba ya kum ba

yah, my Lord, Kum ba yah! Oh, Lord,— Kum ba yah!
ya kum ba ya kum ba ya

2. Come by here, my Lord,
    Kum ba yah!
Come by here, my Lord,
    Kum ba yah!
Come by here, my Lord,
    Kum ba yah!
Oh, Lord, Kum ba yah!

3. Someone's singing, Lord,
    Kum ba yah!
Someone's singing, Lord,
    Kum ba yah!
Someone's singing, Lord,
    Kum ba yah!
Oh, Lord, Kum ba yah!

Pronunciation Guide: "Kum Ba Yah"
a father   u moon

La pequeñita araña
(Eency Weency Spider)

Traditional Rhyme
Arranged by Gilberto Soto

Spanish: La pe - que - ñi - ta a - ra - ña ten - dió su te - la - ra - ña
Pronunciation: la pe ke nyi ta ɾa nya ten dyo su te la ɾa nya

vi - no la llu - via y se la lle - vó.
βi no la yu βya i se la ye βo

Sa - lió el sol y to - do - se se - có y la
sa lyo el sol i to ðo se se ko i la

pe - que - ñi - ta a - ra - ña su - bió, su - bió, su - bió.
pe ke nyi ta ɾa nya su βyo su βyo su βyo

Pronunciation Guide: "La pequeñita araña"

a	f<u>a</u>ther	u	m<u>oo</u>n
e	<u>a</u>pe	β	*b* without lips touching
i	b<u>ee</u>	ð	<u>th</u>e
o	<u>o</u>bey	ɾ	flipped r

London Bridge

Traditional

1. Lon - don Bridge is fall-ing down, fall-ing down, fall-ing down,

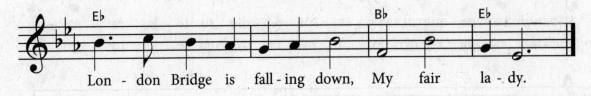

Lon - don Bridge is fall-ing down, My fair la - dy.

2. Build it up with iron bars…

3. Iron bars will bend and break…

4. Build it up with needles and pins…

5. Needles and pins rust and bend…

6. Build it up with silver and gold…

7. Silver and gold I've not got…

Looby Loo

English Singing Game

Refrain

Here we go loo - by loo, Here we go loo - by light,

Here we go loo - by loo, All on a Sat - ur - day night.___

Verse

1.–4. I put my { right / left / right / left } { hand / hand / leg / leg } in,_____ I

take my { right / left / right / left } { hand / hand / leg / leg } out.___ I

give my { hand / hand / leg / leg } a shake, shake, shake, And

Go back to the beginning and sing to end
Da Capo al Fine

turn my - self a - bout. Oh,

Los pollitos
(Little Chickens)

Ecuadorian Folk Song
English Version by MMH

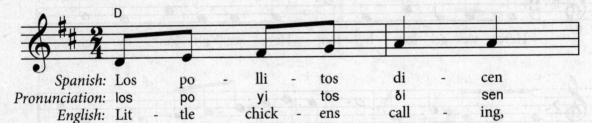

Spanish: Los po - lli - tos di - cen
Pronunciation: los po yi tos ði sen
English: Lit - tle chick - ens call - ing,

"pí - o, pí - o, pí - o"
pi o pi o pi o
"Pí - o, pí - o, pí - o"

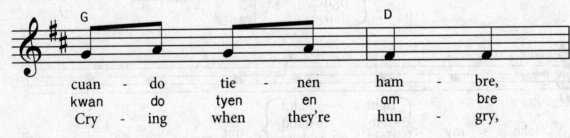

cuan - do tie - nen ham - bre,
kwan do tyen en ɑm bɾe
Cry - ing when they're hun - gry,

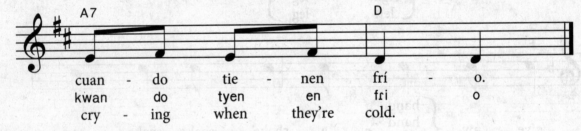

cuan - do tie - nen frí - o.
kwan do tyen en fɾi o
cry - ing when they're cold.

Pronunciation Guide: "Los pollitos"
ɑ f<u>a</u>ther   o <u>o</u>bey
e <u>a</u>pe   ð <u>the</u>
i b<u>ee</u>   ɾ flipped r

Mary Wore Her Red Dress

Virginia Folk Song

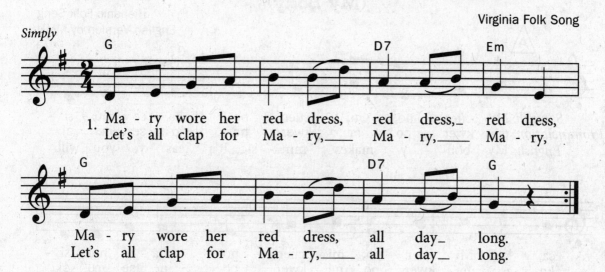

1. Mary wore her red dress, red dress, red dress,
Let's all clap for Mary, Mary, Mary,

Mary wore her red dress, all day long.
Let's all clap for Mary, all day long.

2. Tommy wore a green shirt,...

3. Sadie wore her blue jeans,...

4. Tony wore his yellow boots,...

Merrily, We Roll Along

Traditional Folk Song

Mer - ri - ly, we roll a - long. Roll a - long. Roll a - long.

Mer - ri - ly, we roll a - long. O'er the deep blue sea.

Mi cuerpo
(My Body)

Hispanic Folk Song
English Version by MMH

Spanish: Mi cuer - po, mi cuer - po ha - ce mú - si -
Pronunciation: mi kweɾ po mi kweɾ po ɑ se mu si
English: My bod - y makes mu - sic, It's eas - y, you will

ca, Mi cuer - po, mi cuer - po ha - ce mú - si -
ka mi kweɾ po mi kweɾ po ɑ se mu si
see, My bod - y makes mu - sic, It's eas - y, you will

ca. Mis ma - nos ha - cen (clap clap clap), mis
ka mis mɑ nos ɑ sen mis
see. My hands, my hands go (clap clap clap), My

pi - es ha - cen (stamp stamp stamp), mi bo - ca ha - ce
py es ɑ sen mi βo kɑ ɑ se
feet, my feet go (stamp stamp stamp), My mouth, my mouth goes

"La la la," mi cuer - po ha - ce "Cha cha cha."
mi kweɾ po ɑ se
"La la la," My bod - y does the "Cha cha cha."

Pronunciation Guide: "Mi cuerpo"

ɑ	father	u	moon
e	ape	β	*b* without lips touching
i	bee	ɾ	flipped r
o	obey		

The Muffin Man

Old English Rhyme

1. Oh, do you know the muf - fin man, the
2. Oh, yes I know the muf - fin man, the

muf - fin man, the muf - fin man? Oh,
muf - fin man, the muf - fin man. Oh,

do you know the muf - fin man that
yes, I know the muf - fin man that

lives in Dru - ry Lane?
lives in Dru - ry Lane.

The Mulberry Bush

Game Song

1. Here we go round the mul - ber - ry bush, The mul - ber - ry bush, the mul - ber - ry bush. Here we go round the mul - ber - ry bush So ear - ly in the morn - ing. morn - ing.

2. This is the way we wash our clothes,…
So early Monday morning.

3. This is the way we iron our clothes,…
So early Tuesday morning.

4. This is the way we scrub the floor,…
So early Wednesday morning.

5. This is the way we mend our clothes,…
So early Thursday morning.

6. This is the way we sweep the house,…
So early Friday morning.

7. This is the way we bake our bread,…
So early Saturday morning.

8. This is the way we go to church,…
So early Sunday morning.

My Thumbs Are Starting to Wiggle

Traditional

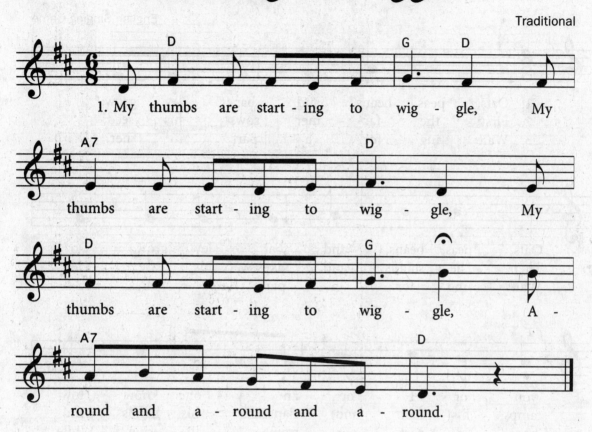

1. My thumbs are start-ing to wig-gle, My thumbs are start-ing to wig-gle, My thumbs are start-ing to wig-gle, A-round and a-round and a-round.

2. …hands…

3. …arms…

4. …legs…

5. *(Faster)* Now all of me is a-wigglin',…

I think I had better sit down.

Oats, Peas, Beans, and Barley Grow

English Singing Game

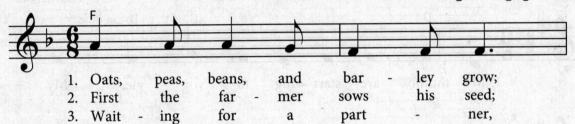

1. Oats, peas, beans, and bar - ley grow;
2. First the far - mer sows his seed;
3. Wait - ing for a part - ner,

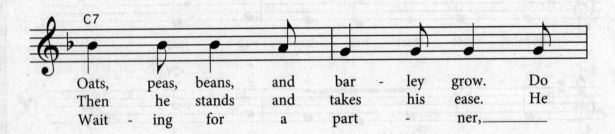

Oats, peas, beans, and bar - ley grow. Do
Then he stands and takes his ease. He
Wait - ing for a part - ner,_____

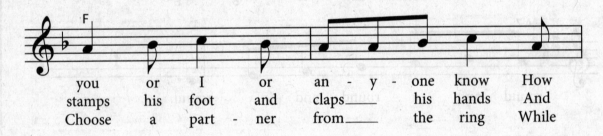

you or I or an - y - one know How
stamps his foot and claps_____ his hands And
Choose a part - ner from_____ the ring While

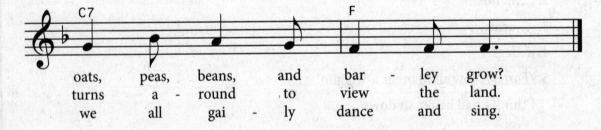

oats, peas, beans, and bar - ley grow?
turns a - round to view the land.
we all gai - ly dance and sing.

Old MacDonald Had a Farm

American Folk Song

1. Old Mac-Don - ald had a farm.

E - I - E - I - O. And on that farm he

had some {
1. chicks.
2. ducks.
3. pigs.
4. cows.
} E - I - E - I - O. With a

*chick, chick here, and a chick, chick there.

(No repeat on Verse 1)

Here a chick, there a chick, Ev - 'ry-where a chick, chick,

Old Mac-Don - ald had a farm. E - I - E - I - O.

*2. …ducks…quack, quack…chick, chick here, chick, chick there…

3. …pigs…oink, oink…quack, quack here, quack, quack there…

4. …cows…moo, moo… moo, moo here, moo, moo there,…

Rain, Rain, Go Away

Traditional Children's Song

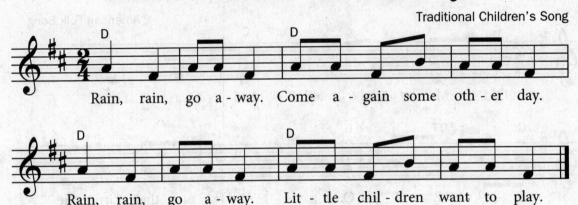

Rain, rain, go a-way. Come a-gain some oth-er day.

Rain, rain, go a-way. Lit-tle chil-dren want to play.

Ring Around the Rosy

English Folk Song

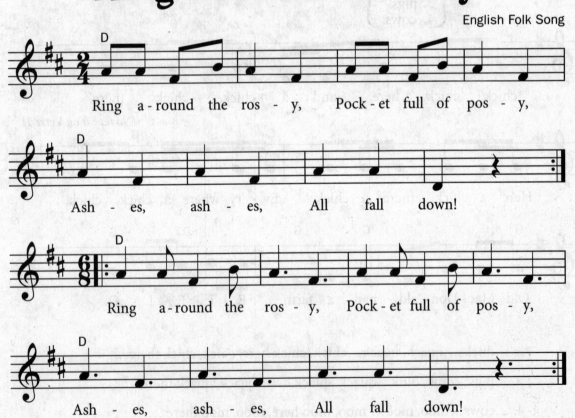

Ring a-round the ros-y, Pock-et full of pos-y,

Ash-es, ash-es, All fall down!

Ring a-round the ros-y, Pock-et full of pos-y,

Ash-es, ash-es, All fall down!

Sally Go 'Round the Sun

Nursery Rhyme

Sal - ly go 'round the { sun._____ / moon._____ }

Sal - ly go 'round the chim - ney tops

Ev - 'ry af - ter - noon. Boom!

Sing a Song of Sixpence

Traditional Nursery Rhyme
Music by J.W. Elliot

Sing a song of six - pence, A pock - et full of rye,

Four and twen - ty black - birds Baked in a pie;

When the pie was o - pened, The birds be - gan to sing,

Was - n't that a dain - ty dish To set be - fore the king?

Six Little Ducks

American Game Song

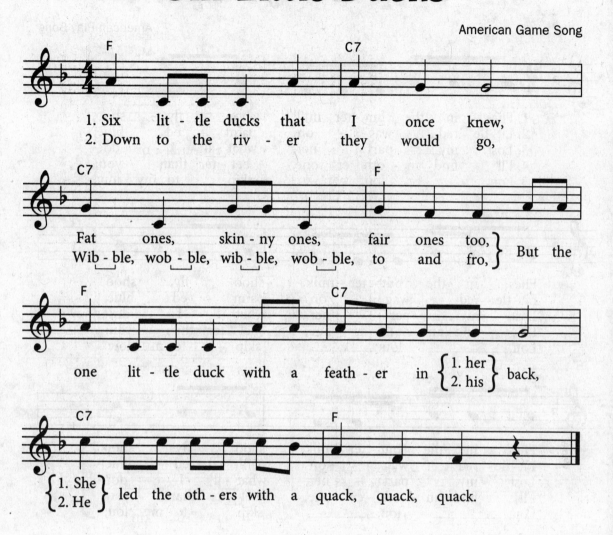

1. Six lit - tle ducks that I once knew,
2. Down to the riv - er they would go,

Fat ones, skin - ny ones, fair ones too,
Wib - ble, wob - ble, wib - ble, wob - ble, to and fro, } But the

one lit - tle duck with a feath - er in { 1. her } back,
{ 2. his }

{ 1. She } led the oth - ers with a quack, quack, quack.
{ 2. He }

Skip to My Lou

American Play Song

1. Flies in the but - ter - milk, shoo fly, shoo,
2. Lit - tle red___ wag - on paint - ed blue;
3. Lost my___ part - ner, what' - ll I do?
4. I'll find an - oth - er one, bet - ter than you;
5. Lou,_____ lou,_____ skip to my lou;

Flies in the but - ter - milk, shoo fly, shoo,
Lit - tle red___ wag - on paint - ed blue;
Lost my___ part - ner, what' - ll I do?
I'll find an - oth - er one, bet - ter than you;
Lou,_____ lou,_____ skip to my lou;

Flies in the but - ter - milk, shoo fly, shoo,
Lit - tle red___ wag - on paint - ed blue;
Lost my___ part - ner, what' - ll I do?
I'll find an - oth - er one, bet - ter than you;
Lou,_____ lou,_____ skip to my lou;

Skip to my lou, my dar - ling.

Song of Thanksgiving

Words and Music by
Robert de Frece

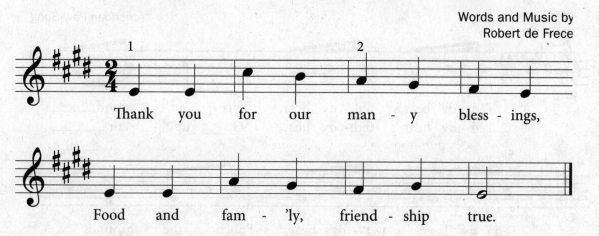

Thank you for our man - y bless - ings,

Food and fam - 'ly, friend - ship true.

Sweetly Sings the Donkey

Traditional

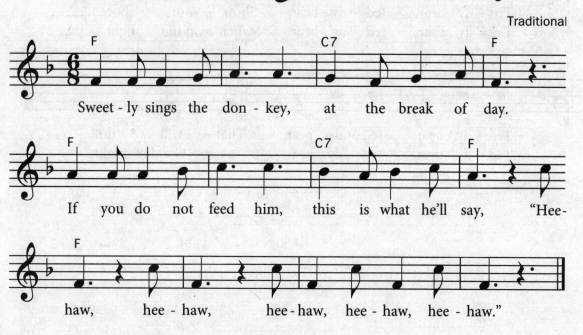

Sweet - ly sings the don - key, at the break of day.

If you do not feed him, this is what he'll say, "Hee-

haw, hee - haw, hee - haw, hee - haw, hee - haw."

Teddy Bear

American Play Song

1. Ted - dy bear, ted - dy bear, Turn a - round. _____
2. Ted - dy bear, ted - dy bear, Go up - stairs. _____

Ted - dy bear, ted - dy bear, Touch the ground.
Ted - dy bear, ted - dy bear, Say your prayers.

Ted - dy bear, ted - dy bear, Show your shoe. _____
Ted - dy bear, ted - dy bear, Switch off the light. _____

Ted - dy bear, ted - dy bear, That will do.
Ted - dy bear, ted - dy bear, Say "Good night."

Ten in a Bed

American Folk Song

6. There were five…

7. There were four…

8. There were three…

9. There were two…

This Is What I Can Do

Children's Singing Game

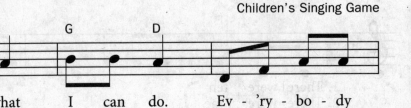

This is what I can do. Ev - 'ry - bo - dy

(Sing 4 times)

do it, too. Now I pass it on to you.

Actions for Interludes

Transportation Version:
- Interlude 1: Drive a car
- Interlude 2: Fly an airplane
- Interlude 3: Toot a boat horn
- Last time: All actions together

Health and Fitness Version:
- Interlude 1: Hop up and down
- Interlude 2: Drop to the ground
- Interlude 3: Crazy Dance (shake arms and shuffle feet)
- Last time: All actions together

This Little Light of Mine

Swing

African American Spiritual

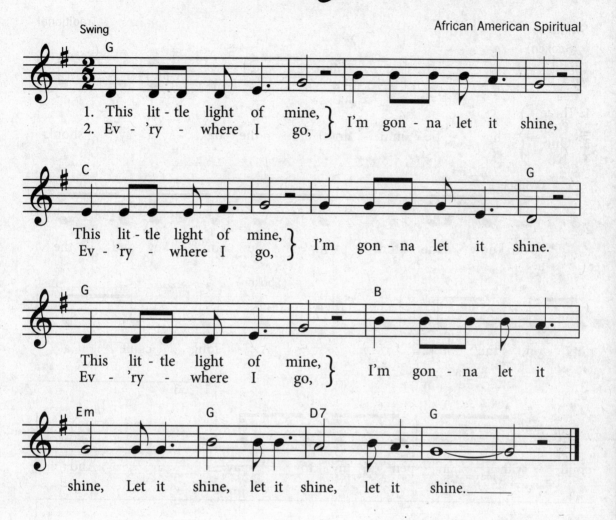

Three Little Muffins

Touch Your Shoulders

Children's Singing Game

Touch your shoul - ders, touch your knees,

Raise your arms and drop them, please.

Touch your an - kles, touch your toes,

Turn a - round and touch your nose.

Twinkle, Twinkle, Little Star

Traditional Children's Song

Twin - kle, twin - kle, lit - tle star, How I won - der what you are,

Up a - bove the world so high, Like a dia - mond in the sky.

Twin - kle, twin - kle, lit - tle star, How I won - der what you are.

We Wish You a Merry Christmas

English Carol

1. We wish you a merry Christmas,
   We wish you a merry Christmas,
   We wish you a merry Christmas,
   And a happy New Year.

2. Now bring us some figgy pudding,
   Now bring us some figgy pudding,
   Now bring us some figgy pudding,
   And bring it out here.

3. For we love our figgy pudding,
   For we love our figgy pudding,
   For we love our figgy pudding,
   So bring some out here.

4. We won't go until we get some,
   We won't go until we get some,
   We won't go until we get some,
   So bring some out here.

5. We wish you a merry Christmas,
   We wish you a merry Christmas,
   We wish you a merry Christmas,
   And a happy New Year.

The Wheels on the Bus

Play Song

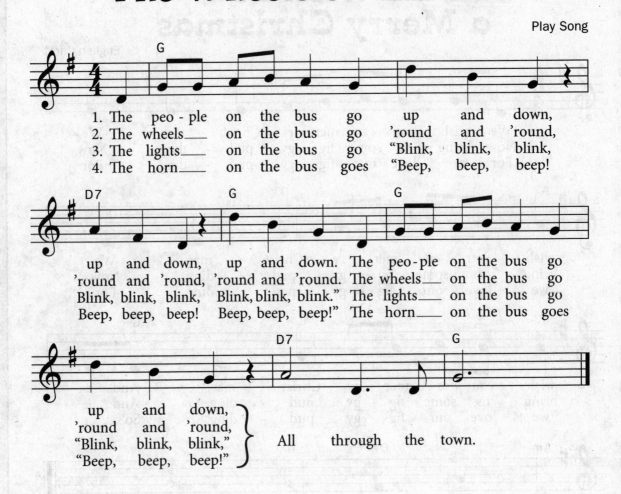

1. The peo-ple on the bus go up and down,
2. The wheels__ on the bus go 'round and 'round,
3. The lights__ on the bus go "Blink, blink, blink,
4. The horn__ on the bus goes "Beep, beep, beep!

up and down, up and down. The peo-ple on the bus go
'round and 'round, 'round and 'round. The wheels__ on the bus go
Blink, blink, blink, Blink, blink, blink." The lights__ on the bus go
Beep, beep, beep! Beep, beep, beep!" The horn__ on the bus goes

up and down,
'round and 'round,
"Blink, blink, blink,"
"Beep, beep, beep!"
} All through the town.

5. The wiper on the bus goes "Swish! Swish! Swish!"

6. The baby on the bus goes "Wah, wah, wah!"

Yankee Doodle

Traditional Melody
Words by Dr. Richard Shuckburgh

1. Fath'r and I went down to camp a -long with Cap - tain
2. Yan - kee Doo - dle went to town, a - rid - ing on a

Good - in', and there we saw the men and boys as
po - ny, He stuck a feath - er in his cap and

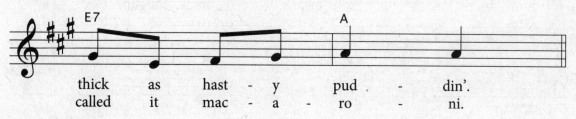

thick as hast - y pud - din'.
called it mac - a - ro - ni.

Refrain

Yan - kee Doo - dle keep it up, Yan - kee Doo - dle dan - dy,

Mind the mu - sic and the step, and with the girls be han - dy.

3. There was Captain Washington upon a slapping stallion,
 a-giving orders to his men; I guess there were a million.

Index

Alphabetical Index of All Titles

1, 2, 3, 4, 5 (rhyme), *111*
1, 2, 3, 4, 5 (song), *124*
1, 2, Buckle My Shoe (rhyme), *110*
1, 2, Buckle My Shoe (song), *125*

A be ce, *126*
Alphabet Song, *127*
America, *128*
America the Beautiful, *129*
Anansi's Dinner Guest, *10*
Apples and Bananas, *130*
Autumn Leaves, *131*

Baa, Baa, Black Sheep, *110*
Bat, The, *118*
Bell Horses, *131*
Bickle, Bockle, *132*
Bingo, *132*
Blow, Wind, Blow!, *109*
Bounce High, Bounce Low, *133*
Bow-Wow, *119*
Boy Who Cried Wolf, The, *14*
Bremen Town Musicians, The, *16*
Brer Rabbit Meets Brer Lion, *20*
Burn Little Candles, *134*
Bye 'n' Bye, *135*

Cinderella, *24*
City Mouse and Country Mouse, *28*
Clap Your Hands, *135*
Clever Jackal, The, *31*
Crocodile and the Hen, The, *35*
Crooked Man, The, *107*

Diddle, Diddle, Dumpling, *104*
Ding, Dong, Bell, *117*

Doctor Foster, *107*
Down at the Station, *136*

Eency Weency Spider, *137*
Engine, Engine, Number Nine, *137*
Farmer in the Dell, The, *138*
Five Fat Turkeys, *139*
Follow Me, *140*
Foolish, Timid Rabbit, The, *37*

Georgy Porgy, *118*
Go a Tin (Lantern Song), *141*
Go Tell It on the Mountain, *141*
Gogo, *142*
Going to St. Ives, *119*
Good Day Song, *143*
Grandmother Spider Brings
the Sun, *40*

Hello Song, *144*
Hey! Diddle, Diddle, *104*
Hickory, Dickory, Dock, *113*
Higglety, Pigglety, Pop (rhyme), *116*
Higglety, Pigglety, Pop (song), *145*
Hoddley, Poddley, *112*
Hokey Pokey, The, *146*
Hop, Hop, Hop, *147*
Hot Cross Buns, *113*
Humpty Dumpty, *112*
Hush, Little Baby, *147*
Hush-a-Bye, *116*

I Wanna Be a Friend of Yours, *148*
If All the Seas, *111*
If All the World Was Paper, *109*
If I Had a Donkey, *107*

If You're Happy, *149*
It's Raining, *108*

Jack and Jill, *104*
Jack and the Beanstalk, *43*
Jack, Be Nimble (rhyme), *119*
Jack, Be Nimble (song), *150*
Jack Sprat, *107*
Jack-a-Nory, *118*
Jingle Bells, *151*
Johnny Cake Boy, The, *47*

Knee-High Man, The, *51*
Kum Ba Yah, *152*

La pequeñita araña (Eency Weency Spider), *153*
Lion and the Mouse, The, *54*
Little Bo-Peep, *112*
Little Boy Blue, *110*
Little Jack Horner, *108*
Little Juan and the Cooking Pot, *56*
Little Miss Muffet, *115*
Little Red Hen, The, *59*
Little Red Riding Hood, *61*
London Bridge, *154*
Looby Loo, *155*
Los pollitos (Little Chickens), *156*

Mary Had a Little Lamb, *111*
Mary, Mary, Quite Contrary, *108*
Mary Wore Her Red Dress, *157*
Merrily, We Roll Along, *157*
Mi cuerpo (My Body), *158*
Mouse Deer Crosses the River, *64*

Muffin Man, The, *159*
Mulberry Bush, The, *160*
My Black Hen, *109*
My Thumbs Are Starting to Wiggle, *161*

North Wind, The, *116*
Now Things Are Worse!, *68*

Oats, Peas, Beans, and Barley Grow, *162*
Old MacDonald Had a Farm, *163*
Old Mother Goose, *104*
Old Mother Hubbard, *114*
Old Woman Who Lived in a Shoe, The, *118*
One Misty, Moisty Morning, *117*
Owl, The, *117*

Pat-a-Cake, *113*
Pease-Porridge Hot, *105*
Peter Piper, *112*
Pie, The, *114*
Polly Put the Kettle On, *108*
Pumpkin Eater, The, *107*
Pussy-Cat, Pussy-Cat, *113*

Rabbit and Coyote's Big Race, *72*
Rain, Rain, Go Away (rhyme), *105*
Rain, Rain, Go Away (song), *164*
Ride Away, Ride Away, *109*
Ring Around the Rosy (rhyme), *116*
Ring Around the Rosy (song), *164*
Rooster Who Went to Tío's Wedding, The, *75*
Roses Are Red, *111*

Sally Go 'Round the Sun, *165*
Simple Simon, *117*
Sing a Song of Sixpence (rhyme), *115*
Sing a Song of Sixpence (song), *166*
Six Little Ducks, *167*
Six Little Mice, *105*
Skip to My Lou, *168*
Song of Thanksgiving, *169*
Star Light, *109*
Sulkey Sue, *114*
Sweetly Sings the Donkey, *169*

Teddy Bear, *170*
Ten in a Bed, *171*
This Is the House That Jack Built, *120*
This Is What I Can Do, *172*
This Little Light of Mine, *173*
Three Bears, The, *79*
Three Billy Goats Gruff, The, *82*
Three Blind Mice, *119*
Three Little Kittens, *106*

Three Little Muffins, *174*
Three Little Pigs, The, *84*
Three Men in a Tub, *114*
Tikki Tikki Tembo, *87*
Timimoto, *91*
To Market, *105*
Tom, Tom, the Piper's Son, *115*
Tommy Tucker, *110*
Tortoise and the Hare, The, *94*
Touch Your Shoulders, *175*
Turtle and the Flute, The, *96*
Tweedledum and Tweedledee, *114*
Twinkle, Twinkle, Little Star, *176*

Voice in Rabbit's House, The, *99*

We Wish You a Merry Christmas, *177*
Wee Willie Winkie, *108*
Wheels on the Bus, The, *178*

Yankee Doodle, *179*

Alphabetical Index of Mother Goose Rhymes

1, 2, 3, 4, 5, *111*
1, 2, Buckle My Shoe, *110*

Baa, Baa, Black Sheep, *110*
Bat, The, *118*
Blow, Wind, Blow!, *109*
Bow-Wow, *119*

Crooked Man, The, *107*

Diddle, Diddle, Dumpling, *104*
Ding, Dong, Bell, *117*
Doctor Foster, *107*

Georgy Porgy, *118*
Going to St. Ives, *119*

Hey! Diddle, Diddle, *104*
Hickory, Dickory, Dock, *113*
Higglety, Pigglety, Pop, *116*
Hoddley, Poddley, *112*
Hot Cross Buns, *113*
Humpty Dumpty, *112*
Hush-a-Bye, *116*

If All the Seas, *111*
If All the World Was Paper, *109*
If I Had a Donkey, *107*
It's Raining, *108*

Jack and Jill, *104*
Jack, Be Nimble, *119*
Jack Sprat, *107*
Jack-a-Nory, *118*

Little Bo-Peep, *112*
Little Boy Blue, *110*
Little Jack Horner, *108*
Little Miss Muffet, *115*

Mary Had a Little Lamb, *111*
Mary, Mary, Quite Contrary, *108*
My Black Hen, *109*

North Wind, The, *116*

Old Mother Goose, *104*
Old Mother Hubbard, *114*
Old Woman, *112*
Old Woman Who Lived in a Shoe, The, *118*
One Misty, Moisty Morning, *117*
Owl, The, *117*

Pat-a-Cake, *113*
Pease-Porridge Hot, *105*
Peter Piper, *112*
Pie, The, *114*
Polly Put the Kettle On, *108*
Pumpkin Eater, The, *107*
Pussy-Cat, Pussy-Cat, *113*

Rain, Rain, Go Away, *105*
Ride Away, Ride Away, *109*
Ring Around the Rosy, *116*
Roses Are Red, *111*

Simple Simon, *117*

Sing a Song of Sixpence, *115*

Six Little Mice, *105*

Star Light, *109*

Sulkey Sue, *114*

This Is the House That Jack Built, *120*

Three Blind Mice, *119*

Three Little Kittens, *106*

Three Men in a Tub, *114*

To Market, *105*

Tom, Tom, the Piper's Son, *115*

Tommy Tucker, *110*

Tweedledum and Tweedledee, *114*

Wee Willie Winkie, *108*

First Line Index of Mother Goose Rhymes

A wise old owl sat in an oak, *117*

As I was going to St. Ives, *119*

Baa, baa, black sheep, *110*

Bat, bat, come under my hat, *118*

Blow, wind, blow! And go, mill, go!, *109*

Bow-wow says the dog, *119*

Diddle, diddle, dumpling, my son John, *104*

Ding, dong, bell, *117*

Doctor Foster went to Gloucester, *107*

Georgy Porgy, pudding and pie, *118*

Here's Sulkey Sue, *114*

Hey! diddle, diddle, *104*

Hickory, dickory, dock, *113*

Higgledy, piggledy, my black hen, *109*

Higglety, pigglety, pop!, *116*

Hoddley, poddley, puddle and fogs, *112*

Hot cross buns! Hot cross buns!, *113*

Humpty Dumpty sat on a wall, *112*

Hush-a-bye, baby, on the treetop, *116*

I'll tell you a story/About Jack-a-Nory, *118*

If all the seas were one sea, *111*

If all the world was paper, *109*

If I had a donkey that wouldn't go, *107*

It's raining, it's pouring, *108*

Jack and Jill went up the hill, *104*

Jack be nimble,/Jack be quick, *119*

Jack Sprat could eat no fat, *107*

Little Bo-Peep has lost her sheep, *112*

Little Boy Blue,/Come blow your horn, *110*

Little Jack Horner/Sat in a corner, *108*

Little Miss Muffet/Sat on a tuffet, *115*

Little Tommy Tucker, *110*

Mary had a little lamb, *111*

Mary, Mary, quite contrary, *108*

Old Mother Goose, *104*

Old Mother Hubbard, *114*

One misty, moisty morning, *117*

One, two, three, four, five, *111*

One, two,/Buckle my shoe, *110*

Pat-a-cake, pat-a-cake, baker's man, *113*

Pease-porridge hot, *105*

Peter Piper picked a peck of pickled peppers, *112*

Peter, Peter, pumpkin eater, *107*

Polly put the kettle on, *108*

Pussy-cat, pussy-cat, where have you been?, *113*

Rain, rain, go away, *105*

Ride away, ride away, *109*

Ring around the rosy, *116*

Roses are red, *111*

Rub-a-dub-dub,/Three men in a tub, *114*

Simple Simon met a pieman, *117*

Sing a song of sixpence, *115*

Six little mice sat down to spin, *105*

The north wind doth blow, *116*

There was a crooked man, *107*

There was an old woman/Lived under a hill, *112*

There was an old woman who lived in a shoe, *118*

This is the house that Jack built, *120*

Three blind mice, see how they run!, *119*

Three little kittens,/They lost their mittens, *106*

To market, to market, to buy a fat pig, *105*

Tom, Tom, the piper's son, *115*

Tweedledum and Tweedledee, *114*

Wee Willie Winkie runs through the town, *108*

Who made the pie?, *114*

Index of Topics

Action

Clap Your Hands, *135*

Gogo, *142*

Hello Song, *144*

Hey! Diddle, Diddle, *104*

Hokey Pokey, The, *146*

Hop, Hop, Hop, *147*

If You're Happy, *149*

Jack, Be Nimble (rhyme), *119*

Jack, Be Nimble (song), *150*

Looby Loo, *155*

My Thumbs Are Starting to Wiggle, *161*

This Is What I Can Do, *172*

Tom, Tom, the Piper's Son, *115*

Touch Your Shoulders, *175*

Wheels on the Bus, The, *178*

Animals

Baa, Baa, Black Sheep, *110*

Bat, The, *118*

Bell Horses, *131*

Bingo, *132*

Bow-Wow, *119*

Ding, Dong, Bell, *117*

Eency Weency Spider, *137*

Farmer in the Dell, The, *138*

Five Fat Turkeys, *139*

Good Day Song, *143*

Hey! Diddle, Diddle, *104*

Hickory, Dickory, Dock, *113*

Higglety, Pigglety, Pop (rhyme), *116*

Higglety, Pigglety, Pop (song), *145*

Hoddley, Poddley, *112*

Hush, Little Baby, *147*

If I Had a Donkey, *107*

La pequeñita araña (Eency Weency Spider), *153*

Little Bo-Peep, *112*

Little Boy Blue, *110*

Little Miss Muffet, *115*

Looby Loo, *155*

Los pollitos (Little Chickens), *156*

Mary Had a Little Lamb, *111*

My Black Hen, *109*

North Wind, The, *116*

Old MacDonald Had a Farm, *163*

Old Mother Goose, *104*

Owl, The, *117*

Pussy-Cat, Pussy-Cat, *113*

Ride Away, Ride Away, *109*

Sing a Song of Sixpence (rhyme), *115*

Sing a Song of Sixpence (song), *166*

Six Little Ducks, *167*

Six Little Mice, *105*

Sweetly Sings the Donkey, *169*

This Is the House That Jack Built, *120*

Three Blind Mice, *119*

Three Little Kittens, *106*

Tom, Tom, the Piper's Son, *115*

Yankee Doodle, *179*

The Body

Clap Your Hands, *135*

Gogo, *142*

Hello Song, *144*

Hokey Pokey, The, *146*

If You're Happy, *149*

Mi cuerpo (My Body), *158*

My Thumbs Are Starting to Wiggle, *161*

Sing a Song of Sixpence (rhyme), *115*

Sing a Song of Sixpence (song), *166*
Touch Your Shoulders, *175*

Clothes
Bat, The, *118*
Diddle, Diddle, Dumpling, *104*
Jack, Be Nimble (song), *150*
Mary Wore Her Red Dress, *157*
Old Woman Who Lived in a Shoe, The, *118*
Six Little Mice, *105*
Three Little Kittens, *106*

Colors
Hello Song, *144*
Hoddley, Poddley, *112*
Little Boy Blue, *110*
Mary Had a Little Lamb, *111*
Mary Wore Her Red Dress, *157*
Merrily, We Roll Along, *157*
Roses Are Red, *111*
Skip to My Lou, *168*

Community
America, *128*
America, the Beautiful, *129*
Blow, Wind, Blow!, *109*
Muffin Man, The, *159*
Simple Simon, *117*
Three Men in a Tub, *114*
To Market, *105*
Wee Willie Winkie, *108*

Counting
1, 2, 3, 4, 5 (rhyme), *111*
1, 2, 3, 4, 5 (song), *124*
1, 2, Buckle My Shoe (rhyme), *110*
1, 2, Buckle My Shoe (song), *125*
Bell Horses, *131*
Bye 'n' Bye, *135*
Engine, Engine, Number Nine, *137*
Five Fat Turkeys, *139*
Going to St. Ives, *119*
Hickory, Dickory, Dock, *113*
Hot Cross Buns, *113*
Sing a Song of Sixpence (rhyme), *115*
Sing a Song of Sixpence (song), *166*
Six Little Ducks, *167*
Ten in a Bed, *171*
Three Blind Mice, *119*
Three Little Kittens, *106*
Three Little Muffins, *174*

Family
Diddle, Diddle, Dumpling, *104*
Hot Cross Buns, *113*
Jack Sprat, *107*
Jack-a-Nory, *118*
Old Woman Who Lived in a Shoe, The, *118*
Ride Away, Ride Away, *109*

Farm Life
Baa, Baa, Black Sheep, *110*
Bingo, *132*
Blow, Wind, Blow!, *109*
Farmer in the Dell, The, *138*
Little Bo-Peep, *112*

Little Boy Blue, *110*

Los pollitos (Little Chickens), *156*

My Black Hen, *109*

Oats, Peas, Beans, and Barley Grow, *162*

Old MacDonald Had a Farm, *163*

Food

Apples and Bananas, *130*

Bat, The, *118*

Blow, Wind, Blow!, *109*

Hot Cross Buns, *113*

Jack Sprat, *107*

Little Jack Horner, *108*

Little Miss Muffet, *115*

Muffin Man, The, *159*

Oats, Peas, Beans, and Barley Grow, *162*

Old Woman Who Lived in a Shoe, The, *118*

Pat-a-Cake, *113*

Pease-Porridge Hot, *105*

Pie, The, *114*

Polly Put the Kettle On, *108*

Pumpkin Eater, The, *107*

Simple Simon, *117*

Sing a Song of Sixpence (rhyme), *115*

Sing a Song of Sixpence (song), *166*

Skip to My Lou, *168*

Three Little Kittens, *106*

Three Little Muffins, *174*

Tommy Tucker, *110*

Pets

Bingo, *132*

Ding, Dong, Bell, *117*

If I Had a Donkey, *107*

Mary Had a Little Lamb, *111*

My Black Hen, *109*

Old Mother Hubbard, *114*

Ride Away, Ride Away, *109*

Plants and Gardens

Autumn Leaves, *131*

Mary, Mary, Quite Contrary, *108*

Mulberry Bush, The, *160*

Oats, Peas, Beans, and Barley Grow, *162*

Peter Piper, *112*

Ring Around the Rosy (rhyme), *116*

Ring Around the Rosy (song), *164*

Roses Are Red, *111*

Seasons and Holidays

Autumn Leaves, *131*

Burn Little Candles, *134*

Jingle Bells, *151*

Little Jack Horner, *108*

Song of Thanksgiving, *169*

We Wish You a Merry Christmas, *177*

The Sky

Bye 'n' Bye, *135*

Sally Go 'Round the Sun, *165*

Star Light, *109*

Twinkle, Twinkle, Little Star, *176*

Transportation

Down at the Station, *136*

Engine, Engine, Number Nine, *137*

Merrily, We Roll Along, *157*

Ride Away, Ride Away, *109*

Three Men in a Tub, *114*

Wheels on the Bus, The, *178*

Yankee Doodle, *179*

Transition Songs

Bickle, Bockle, *132*

Bounce High, Bounce Low, *133*

Follow Me, *140*

This Is What I Can Do, *172*

Touch Your Shoulders, *175*

Weather

Autumn Leaves, *131*

Doctor Foster, *107*

Eency Weency Spider, *137*

It's Raining, *108*

La pequeñita araña (Eency Weency Spider), *153*

North Wind, The, *116*

One Misty, Moisty Morning, *117*

Rain, Rain, Go Away (rhyme), *105*

Rain, Rain, Go Away (song), *164*

Credits and Acknowledgements

Songs:

The Hokey Pokey Words and Music by Charles P. Macak, Tafft Baker and Larry La Prise Copyright © 1950 Sony/ATV Songs LLC Copyright renewed. All Rights Reserved. Administered by Song/ATV Music Publishing, 8 Music Square West, Nashville, TN 37203. International Copyright secured. All Rights Reserved.

Song of Thanksgiving Words and Music by Robert de Frece Copyright © 2001 BELWIN-MILLS PUBLISHING CORP. All Rights Reserved. Used by Permission.

Cover illustration: Oleynikov

Illustration credits: Liisa Chauncy Guida, 3; Nicole in den Bosch, 3; Marcy Ramsey, 3; Brian Lies, 3; Nan Brooks, 4; Irana Shepherd, 4; Paige Billin-Frye, 4; Carol Schwartz, 4; R.W. Alley, 5; Lynne Cravath, 5; Jayoung Cho, 6; Mary Newell DePalma, 6; Bonnie Matthews, 7; Carol Schwartz, 7; Irana Shepherd, 7; Fabricio Vanden Broeck, 10–13; Kate Flanagan, 14–15; Liisa Chauncy Guida, 16–19; Teri Weidner, 20–23; Nicole in den Bosch, 24–27; Amy Huntington, 28–30; Erin Eitter-Kono, 31–34; Kate Flanagan, 35–36; Mary Newell DePalma, 37–39; Ruth Flanigan, 40–42; Marcy Ramsey, 43–47; Jayoung Cho, 48–50; Brian Lies, 51–53; Ashley Mims, 54–55; Rosario Valderrama, 56–58; Kelly Murphy, 59–60; Carol Schwartz, 61–63; Terri Murphy, 64–67; R.W. Alley, 68–71; Irana Shepherd, 72–74; Kathy Wilburn, 75–78; Kate Flanagan, 79–81; Carol Schwartz, 82–83; Nicole in den Bosch, 84–86; Hector Borlasca, 87–91; Chi Chung, 91–93; Doug Panton, 95–95; Gerardo Suzan, 96–98; Randy Chewning, 99–101; Nan Brooks, 104; Bonnie Matthews, 105; Irana Shepherd, 106; Paige Billin-Frye, 107; Jayoung Cho, 108; Cary Pillo, 109; Jean Cassels, 110; Carol Schwartz, 111; Teri Weidner, 112; Lynne Cravath, 113; Kate Flanagan, 114; R.W. Alley, 115; Mary Newell DePalma, 116; Teri Weidner, 117; Bonnie Matthews, 118; Jayoung Cho, 119; Carol Schwartz, 120–121; Nicole in den Bosch, 181; Gerardo Suzan, 184; R.W. Alley, 186; Jean Cassels, 188